CAGES
OF
PAIN

CAGES OF PAIN

GORDON AESCHLIMAN

WORD PUBLISHING
Dallas · London · Vancouver · Melbourne

CAGES OF PAIN: HOPE FOR VICTIMS OF RELIGION

Library of Congress Cataloging-in-Publication Data

Aeschliman, Gordon D., 1975–
    Cages of pain : hope for victims of religion / by Gordon Aeschliman.
      p. cm.
    ISBN 0–8499–3273–4
    1. Young adults—Religious life.   I. Title.
  BV4529.2.A37   1991
  248.8'4—dc20   91–19082
                                             CIP

Printed in the United States of America

1 2 3 4 9 LB 9 8 7 6 5 4 3 2 1

to tom w.

Contents

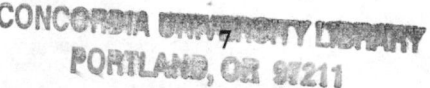

Foreword

I needed this book. I needed its message. I needed its hope. I needed its Dionysian form of spirituality that inspires us to laugh at our foibles, to sing praises to God in the midst of our sufferings, and to dance away from those who would try to squeeze us into their little boxes.

This book is a description of what has happened to those of us who have an ambivalent relationship with the church. As such I can easily follow its message. It is a book for people who have trusted the church with their hopes and dreams only to end up disillusioned and hurt. Its message is for those of us who have found out too late that there are many households of faith that are more likely to *use* us than to *love* us.

If your way of handling the pains of betrayal and exploitation experienced in your encounters with Christendom is to try to forget them, then this book is definitely not for you. The vivid illustrations and descriptions of what this man and his friends have endured will conjure up memories of events and experiences that have long been repressed. This book is only for those who believe that honesty about what has really happened is the beginning of healing.

This is not a book that can be summarized by a simple reciting of the verse "All things work together for good for those who love God and are called according to his purpose" (Romans 8:28) in the face of the tragedies of life. Gordon Aeschliman by no means offers easy explanations for why bad things happen to good people. Here you will find that the tragedies and pains we encounter are not rationalized away with those pietistic explanations that never do ring true. Instead of being offered a theology to explain our sufferings, we are introduced to the Person who has endured all that we endure and can teach us how to live through our sufferings to Joy.

There is evil in the world, and that evil produces absurdities that do not easily fit into a divine plan of goodness. Aeschliman does not pretend that they do. He does not believe in a God who makes everything OK. Instead, he introduces us to a God who suffers and overcomes sufferings, is hurt and overcomes hurt, is wronged and forgives, and is crucified but rises again. This God, revealed in Jesus, tells us that what he did we can do also, because he empowers us with his Spirit.

This book does not reduce the problem of evil to a theology. Instead, it is a call to learn to live in triumph and hope through the counsel and love of the Son of God. If there was ever a time you felt like asking, "With a church like this, who needs Satan?" you will relate to what is in these pages. But let me assure you that Aeschliman is no cynic. He still believes in the church and its mission. He is still convinced that the church is the bride of Christ. He still contends that this church is the primary instrument through which God builds the kingdom of heaven here on earth.

He makes us look at the church as it is. He helps us adjust to its shortcomings, and he invites us to work for its greater glory. Now that is a lot to say for any book, but that is what this book is about. I kid you not!

TONY CAMPOLO

Front Notes

The story of persecution in the early church is quoted with permission from the excellent book *Blessed Are the Persecuted*, by Ivo Lesbaupin (Orbis, 1987); Kari Torjesen Malcom's wonderful book *Women at the Crossroads* (InterVarsity Press) is my source on the brave New England women; Nico Smith's story appeared in an earlier book of mine, *Apartheid: Tragedy in Black and White* (Regal); C. S. Lewis' words on the human worth come from *The Weight of Glory, Transposition, and Other Addresses,* © 1949 C.S. Lewis Pty. Ltd. (Harper Collins); the lyrics to "This Is Your Life" come from the album *Red Moon,* by The Call (© 1990 by Neeb Music); and, finally, a few of the thoughts in this book are adaptations from editorials I wrote in various issues of *World Christian* magazine.

Weanling

I press my despair against
    her breasts
But it's poison I drink there
And stagger I drunk cursing
    the loneliness in my wretched
    frame that finds no rest
    in choices cruelly laughed
    at this desperate one

The night is darker than you
    know and the light does
    not come

Passion meets fire and burns its
    rage furiously into the
    silence till ashes are blown
    leaving only distance in
    the cavern of separation

Uncharted vacuums offer their
    hollow comfort and the moon
    sinks behind the exit to
    hell

Turn south. Gallop your panic
    toward the parched plain
    that rips at your dry
    throat and crushes your
    suffocating lungs

Veer west. Face the formidable
    range that promises gold
    and leaves its fools buried
    in the dust of dreams
    forbidden

Run now. Reach north, you say.
    Grasp at the virgin expanse
    that chills your heart and
    mocks your thoughts of
    intimacy

Go east. Return to what was and
    look for the familiar. But
    watch your soul shrivel in
    the retreat to what cannot
    satisfy your hunger

No, orphan child, you are alone

Climb inside your desolation.
Scream your pain and flex
    with all your strength as
    you throw your precious
    self against the farthest
    membrane of the universe

Listen for the colors of spring,
    if you can
But do not look.

Gordon Aeschliman

PART ONE

Cages of Pain

1

The Dark Side of Love

There is no easy answer for their pain.

Following Jesus is supposed to be good for us, yet all too often Christians who have risked the most for Jesus are those who now endure a desperately agonizing existence marked by betrayal, loneliness, confusion, and darkness. God, it's so tormenting inside that downward spiral of despair.

You can find them almost anywhere: people who became vulnerable to the irresistible pull of love's call and are now crushed as a consequence. Sincerity, idealism, passion, caring—name it what you will, these people were motivated to give themselves selflessly to others, to love their neighbors as themselves.

Love took on many expressions—feeding the hungry, church planting among super-resistant Muslims, struggling to free those trapped under the tyranny of oppressive governments, creatively working to interrupt the cycle of poverty that imprisons generation after generation of urban poor, patiently slogging through the jungle of emotions with teenage victims of sexual abuse and dysfunctional families.

The reward for these love-givers was not the miracle of changed lives and grateful hearts. On the contrary, their efforts were rewarded with estrangement from the closest of family members, biting criticism, firing from ministry positions, bankruptcy, and divorce. What was once the vanguard of gentle, tender, sacrificial servants became a bedraggled company of wonderful people who are now prisoners of compassion.

Integrity requires us to reject the simple answers and mindless rehearsal of Bible verses that so easily flow from the mouths of those who have not slogged through the vulnerable territory of passionate loving. A dreadful darkness and unutterable pain have become the companions of these angels of mercy, and our insensitive verbal prescriptions only move them further down the tunnel of despair. The old rules, pop-up verses, and prepackaged words of comfort bring no healing to these victims of religion.

Sometimes because of life's circumstances, I too have stood at the cliff's edge of that valley of pain. I have been consumed in those moments by fear, a gripping panic that I was only a breath's nudge away from falling. And sometimes I have been tempted in the agony of those moments to step over the edge and lose myself fully in the pain. Complete darkness appeared a more welcome friend than the call to stay in the unbearable light.

Some may think me crazy to paint a picture of such ravaging hopelessness. I say such people have never entered into the fellowship of Jesus, who screamed in the agony of giving, "My God, my God, why have you forsaken me?" And a darkness covered the earth.

If you are reading this book, perhaps it is because you too have often screamed out those pleading words in a frantic, last-ditch prayer for relief. It's been the prayer of my trampled heart all too often, and my guess is it's been the same for you. Tune out the voices of those insensitive religious people who so easily belittle your pain—those "mature" Christian men and women who have known nothing but the "joy of the Lord." For them the harshest of words are reserved: They're either liars or deluded lunatics who years ago bought a ticket to Disneyland and never found the way out. Their words are poison to the sickhearted, chains for the downtrodden.

I have discovered that there is a place of tenderness, a certain quiet-in-the-soul. It's not a place of words, of lofty doctrinal formulas that readily dismiss the age-old "problem of pain." No, the sanctuary I have found is a world of laughter, of grief, of companionship—a ridiculous peace that stubbornly lunges at pain and wrestles it to the ground in an uncontested pin; it's a village at dance till two in the morning even though six o'clock marks the hour of departure for another day of body-wrenching labor in the oppressor's manufacturing plant.

Several years ago a friend and I started a little volunteer ministry in Mexico called "Potter's Clay." We were students at Westmont College, and the idea was to create both an opportunity for exposure to another culture and a shot at hands-on ministry. The program became so popular that more than a third of the student body would (and still does) spend the Easter break in Ensenada. Two years ago I was invited to join the students on the annual sojourn and lead the morning chapels. I had missed out on the fun for several years prior; now, as I arrived and surveyed the scene, a familiar sense of anticipation rose up in me. Tents crowded each other into the little flat next to the riverbed that twenty-four hours earlier had been dry. Predictably, the night before the uninitiated students had chosen the lower, more spacious territory, only to be completely washed out by the inevitable torrents of rain. Mess tent, guitar music, laughter, and outhouses: It all promised to be a good week.

The next day's events mocked our laughter and ripped at our hearts. I still carry the pain of those wounds.

A team of five students on the way to their work project breathed in the beauty of Highway D1, hugging the Ensenada coast. Morning mist, Giant Island, splashing waves, and excited chatter in anticipation of another round of giving were brutally interrupted by the split-second visual clip of an airborne Ford LTD crashing into their tiny vehicle's windshield.

Metal strikes metal, each slamming against the other's fifty-five-miles-per-hour force. Engines dislodge, a roof is shaved off as if it were morning stubble, iron twists and snaps. Bodies frantically reach for the light as darkness presses in.

Who can describe the next eight hours of scrambling to save lives? Dear Jesus, I've never heard such prayers. I planted myself in the emergency room at General, where three of the students were transported. The other two were taken to Social Security Hospital. Lisa's limp frame lay helplessly in the corner, pulsating in rhythm with the life-support systems. Brain dead. Three nurses stood around her like merciful angels about a child-at-dreams.

Patti's conscious mind fought piercing stabs of pain from crushed bones, ripped muscles, and a broken back. Her ears took in the sounds of medics fighting to save Garth, just three feet from her gurney. Both Garth and Alan (over at Security) needed blood for surgery. Outside, students pleaded with Mexican pedestrians to test and donate. The local people's instant and sympathetic response was matched only by that of the doctors who also gave their blood—while in surgery. Several operations later, in the early afternoon, we lost Alan. He was transported to the city morgue, and the pain of his passing was soon exacerbated by the legal battles of moving his body across an international border. Lisa was flown to San Diego, where her parents would face cruel and disquieting choices. Patti was ambulanced across the border; her body is still working toward recovery.

Garth and Megan were too unstable for immediate transfer to the United States. Emergency aircraft waited twenty minutes away at the military base. Both of them underwent several operations and in a fragile moment of apparent strength were sirened off to the planes. The ambulance ride seemed to take forever, and as the planes stretched for altitude and circled north, we collapsed on the tar-mac and sobbed our hopelessness. Megan lived.

Last year I visited the memorial altar of stones that all five hundred students built in Ensenada the day after the accident. No picket fences or green grass to mark off the loss of our friends, just the familiar drab river rocks pinning down dried red roses from a year before, as if to remind us of the crushing of our loves—their lives taken in the act of giving. I wished to God I had never started Potter's Clay. The dance of pain. And as my body heaved with a year's worth of wrestling and tears, I was held upright in the arms of my pastor friend, who offered no words, but silently and simply enlarged a place of tenderness within me.

Does the pain go away? No, but thankfully it is often diminished. And then it comes crashing in once again, and the horror is relived in absolute clarity and perfect sequence. You are caught up in a passionate plea that they will not die—but then something, perhaps a scurrying cat, brings your thoughts back to the present, and you remember that they're already dead. It happened again to me tonight: a wonderful walk on a pitch-dark country lane with the first rain of fall washing against my face. The horizon was torn, suddenly, by the rotating lights and blaring sirens of three ambulances, two police cars, and two fire engines that rushed past me, then over the hill.

Damn the darkness. Since when are we supposed to find good in the savage deeds of hell?

I will never forget the wailing of a Christian Ethiopian mother who early one morning, before the sun rose, presented her dead daughter to me. Her shrill scream pierced the foggy quiet of that vast Ethiopian plain as she begged me to mend what I could not. Barely clothed herself, her body wracked with famine, this mother had suffered a loss that was not simply another statistic to be recorded in the United Nations' annual summary of world hunger. How could she be comforted? Her loss was irrevocable, devastating, final.

The passing of children inflicts such violence on the soul.

When Keith Green was killed, two of his children went with him. That morning Don Burmeister, shuttle pilot for Last Days Ministries, flew me from Dallas/Fort Worth to Lindale. Keith and I spent the better part of the day finalizing details to merge our two organizations. We had been dreaming for quite some time of how the combined strengths of music and writing could be used to nurture a call to compassionate living in hundreds of thousands of youth already touched by Keith's unusual talent and sacrificial spirit. "The Lord has given me a mission for the rest of my life," Keith told me that afternoon in his studio. "It's to call youth to go into all the world with Jesus' love."

It all seemed too wonderful to be true, and our plotting turned to giggling like that of a couple of boys who have made off with Grandma's cookie jar and are now behind the barn devouring the booty. We skimmed some of Keith's library books on revival (he was convinced that all service should flow from a deep, personal, loving relationship with Jesus), and then he played me some songs he was composing. The piano had been professionally tuned just that afternoon, and, of course, we had no way of knowing this would be Keith's final concert.

Late that afternoon, the Smalleys, a family of eight from Los Angeles, arrived en route to the East Coast, where they hoped to plant a church. Friends of Keith and Melody, they were a wonderful story of success: healthy, committed Christians who had started in the gutter and trudged their way through several failures in their sincere efforts to follow Jesus. And now they wanted to share this life with others.

We all decided to go for a quick tour of the area in Last Days' airplane. Don took the controls, and passengers took their seats. Two of Keith's kids wanted to go along, so I relinquished my spot, knowing I would get my turn the next day. We stood back as the twin engines wound up for the sprint.

Seconds after takeoff the plane dropped to the ground and exploded. The fire scorched us with menacing licks of flame. It was not until a half-hour later that we were able to make out the twelve forms of what once were friends and loves. And sickened, we had to stand by as the local volunteer fire force unceremoniously hosed down the charred remains so that we could lay them to rest in body bags without burning our hands. Believe me, we would have preferred the charred hands.

Zipping shut a body bag is as clear as death gets, and that evening we locked the pain in our hearts.

In the morning we all gathered under the care of revivalist Leonard Ravenhill. I shall always carry with me his tender description of the tameless Keith, who had known Jesus for seven years but served as though he had followed him for seventy. Then, in faith, we sang the hymn:

When peace like a river attendeth my way,
When sorrows like sea billows roll,
Whatever my lot, thou hast taught me to say:
It is well, it is well with my soul.

It was more of a plea than a statement, for those sea billows had taken with them our friends and dreams. It's been eight years, and I still cry every time I hear that hymn.

A few feet away from me, a pregnant widow sat cross-legged on the floor, her head swaying to the music and her long hair sweeping the carpet as if to wash the feet of Jesus. Her tears were a wrenchingly pungent perfume.

The dark side of love. My God, how it oppresses. You have said you will not break a bruised reed. Why do there seem to be so many broken? Please rescue us. Please shine your light in our dark places. Smash our chains. Rip our prison doors from their hinges. Take us to the place of tenderness, and heal the savage gashes in our hearts.

2

The Prison of Our Soul

Where can we run to escape the cruel assault on our innocence?

Michelle thought it would be the church. By the age of twenty-four, she had become trapped in the demeaning world of prostitution, drug addiction, and alcoholism. What had begun as a harmless (she thought) contract to dance at a local nightclub turned out to be a one-way road into the clutches of a pimp. Michelle was forced into drug use. As her addiction developed, the pimp had less need for his tactics of intimidation, for now her body demanded that she return every night to the source of her relief. And the source of her hell.

Every night Michelle's body and emotions suffered the onslaught of men who used her to massage their lust. A few frenzied minutes and ten dollars later, she was discarded on the sheets for the next animal-in-heat. Sleep would come just before sunrise, and breakfast at noon was coffee strengthened with a shot of tequila. At dinnertime, an escort provided by the pimp drove her to work, where she handed over the cash, disappeared down chemical lane, and numbed her mind for the next round of degradation.

This is not the sort of job in which you can give your two-weeks' notice. Threats and beatings are the personnel policy of this world, and Michelle had seen the treatment meted out to other women who tried to escape the bondage. A sense of dignity and a desperation to be whole, however, won out in Michelle's struggle against fear. She disguised herself and hid for several days while going through withdrawal. The terror of being found by her pimp and her body's violent protests against cold turkey were Michelle's only companions for what felt like an eternity. Finally a calm settled in, and she began to plot her trip to anonymity.

Life is not so kind. She was discovered and dragged into the chambers of the raging pimp, who beat her with his iron-hammer fists until she slumped to the ground in unconscious surrender. Other prostitutes who had been exhibiting only a tentative commitment to their duties sat through the required seminar.

When Michelle woke, she immediately recognized the friendly chemical working its way through her web of arteries, and she allowed herself the relief it offered her crushed spirit. That night she obediently saddled up once again, and a dozen men rode her till sunrise.

Suicide seemed a welcome final off-ramp from Michelle's wretched road, and soon once again she lay unconscious on the floor. Pools of blood formed from the deep decisive cuts on each wrist. But cruelty again mocked her attempted escape from hell: A relative discovered Michelle on the kitchen floor, and an ambulance rushed to interrupt the flow of blood and the flight to freedom.

This time Michelle dragged herself to the courts of the loving Christ. Few of us make our first entry to the church under such conditions. Michelle had no self-worth left. She was the soiled rag of men's pleasures, and she had even failed in taking her own life. She came to God's sanctuary pleading and broken. You learn as a prostitute to grovel in the presence of authority, and so she did in the presence of God, vulnerable as a disobedient dog that cowers in wait for the master's sentence. Will it be mercy or will it be punishment?

For Michelle it was punishment: Halfway through the church service the pastor recognized her. Before the entire congregation, he lectured Michelle for defiling the house of God with her filthy presence and ordered her out. This time the punishment penetrated deeper than men's violation, deeper than the humiliation of the pimp's seminar. Michelle's very soul had been violated by God, and the only life left to her now was one in which the human spirit does not exist.

No, God is not dead. Michelle knew better than that. She had seen the living God in his courts, and there he condemned her soul to everlasting hell. She lived, but what lived was a vacant body and cauterized emotions.

This is the Michelle I met. Her vacuous eyes locked onto my gaze from across the room as her body writhed through a pitiful dance of invitation to the flesh-hungry men who crowded around her, anticipating the show's climax in the bedroom. After the band wound up its tinny finale and men took their numbers, Michelle came over to my table and went through the litany of lies. "Your eyes are so beautiful. I can tell you are a wonderful man and I know I could be happy with you." She had returned voluntarily to this world where you can live if your soul is dead. A couple lies, a few dollars, and animal meets animal.

A friend and I visited Michelle several evenings in a row, and finally she asked us why it was we just talked with her and didn't ask for her services. We responded that we wanted her to know about Jesus. We had no idea what history lay behind her venomous response to our notion that God loves the soul.

Michelle had gone sincerely and innocently to the church for help. Her fragile spirit had been finally crushed in that experience, because she had understood that God is head of the church—consequently, she had trusted the people of the church with her battered soul. Their rejection of her—or should I put it in more honest terms? their outrageous and pharisaical abuse of her trust—had locked her soul in prison. The church was the only spiritual authority she knew, and so her soul remained under its lock and key. And the chief prison guard was the pastor.

I have lost count of the number of people I have met across the United Sates for whom the church is the prison of their soul. Perhaps you are one of them.

You have been abused, slighted, betrayed, cast out, cheated on, chopped up and discarded. And it was not done by some grisly beast whose very appearance warned you to be on guard. No, you gave your trust to the local youth pastor, the mission committee, the elders, the folk in charge of your spiritual well-being, or the board members of your ministry.

Your holy of holies has been violated, and the scandalous fact is that it was done by the church.

How to navigate through this betrayal is not clear. Guilt, anger, listlessness, rage, confusion, and loneliness are your company. You live in a cage of pain, trapped in part by your loyalty to and the authority you confer upon those who have abused you. You suffer in a prison whose architects and builders are the very people who were supposed to look after your soul.

We wonder: How could they have done that to me after all I sacrificed for them? Why am I being punished for trying to do right? Why did she seem so committed to destroying me? Whom *can* I trust? They were my friends—where do I go now? Do I deserve what he did to me, somehow bring it upon myself?

And then these questions inevitably shift to our relationship with God: Why did the Lord do this to me? After all I sacrificed for God's clear call on my life, why am I being punished? Why did God not protect me from that pastor? Perhaps God does not truly love me.

Lisa's story is all too common. At the age of thirteen, she shone among her peers in the youth group. Making friends was no problem because her beauty had boosted her confidence from even a much earlier age. She was now experiencing the changes of puberty and was in fact well ahead of schedule in her physical development.

Her church is a large evangelical congregation, the leader of religious activities in the community. Local pastors wish they could have a shot at that congregation, where there is such a wonderful spirit of giving, the mission budget is unusually high, evangelism thrives, and packed-out seminars on everything from church growth to successful marriages are hosted every month.

The youth group is a model of community outreach. Kids seem to want to attend the church's events more than they do the wild neighborhood parties. Even the local newspaper, normally hostile to "fundamentalists," finds it necessary from time to time to throw in its voice of support for the church's positive impact on the town. The youth pastor, Jeremy, was himself a product of the church's much-hailed discipleship program and was going on eleven years of heading up the youth department.

Jeremy noticed that Lisa had changed. It was not until much later that Lisa realized that his praise of her leadership qualities had very little to do with her skills—Jeremy wanted to be around her. Her unsuspecting young mind saw only a spiritual leader whom she genuinely admired and a man who seemed very happy in his marriage (he loved to describe it in the church seminars). Several times Lisa had done child care for his two young sons, and she thought that Jeremy's wife would be a good model for her to follow.

Lisa's leadership gifts meant that she was called upon to engage in long, personal Bible studies with Jeremy. Their shared duties usually included cleanup after youth group and, once everyone else was gone, a review of plans for the next week. One very late Tuesday evening when all the church was locked up, Jeremy and Lisa were playfully chasing each other around the supplies room, as they seemed to do more often lately, and unexpectedly she found herself caught in his embrace against the counter next to the janitor's sink. There were some giggles, the brushing of hair from her face, and a sequence of moves that ended in rape, although Lisa's confused thirteen-year-old mind believed the youth pastor's words that it was really quite natural and helpful to his personal needs. She also trusted his caution that nobody should hear of it.

"It" never happened again, and Lisa soon found her leadership role being diminished. Her confusion deepened, and it was not until two years later that she understood Jeremy's deed for what it was. She found the courage to confront him. Jeremy responded in anger: She had knowingly and viciously seduced him, throwing all his years of ministry and marriage into jeopardy. Fortunately for her, God had intervened and saved them both. She could expect God's judgment if she pursued the matter any further.

Well, who wants God's wrath? For the next seven years Lisa lived with the guilt of having seduced God's chosen servant. The keeper of her soul's prison was, of course, Jeremy.

The real stories just do not end: Ministry leaders are dumped without a caring process, a young pastor is abruptly discarded for not meeting a powerful elder's expectations, a quick vote brings to an end the years of careful service and giving of a senior staff member, malicious rumors harm the public integrity of one who falls victim to an upstart's eye on position, promises are not kept to a family that crosses several state lines to help manage a non-profit church-planting ministry, the contract is broken between a large Christian record company and a young aspiring musician, a professor at a Christian college is denied tenure because of her colleagues' jealousy.

Very few of the people who have recounted their crippling stories to me have found comfort from Christians around them. One described it as lying on the operating table in excruciating pain after being run over by a semi truck. The surgeon pokes away at the holes and gashes in your body and lectures you for being in a position that left you vulnerable to semi trucks. Meanwhile, you're bleeding to death.

Some tell how their pain is belittled by others who speak paternalistically of the need to "snap out of it: Real Christians get up and go on with life." Others, like Lisa, tell how they not only have been abused, victims of others' sins, but are also being blamed for the events that led to their pain.

And if that is not enough, they are encouraged to find the good they can learn from the experience. What sort of twisted being would look for the good lesson in rape? Some would make light of the violation suffered by these wounded ones. But spiritual rape is exactly what it is. The priest plunged the parishioner.

The most debilitating aspect of these abuses is that they have come at the hands of those in whom you had vested spiritual authority; that is the prime, if not the only, reason your soul is in their prison. Too often, well-meaning friends do not understand that the very core of your life has been violated and that you now face an arduous and painful journey back to the real sanctuary of God. You are so dismayed, confused, and listless, so without hope, that you don't really expect to find an oasis for your soul. You suspect that you are going to end up accepting some abstract doctrinal resolution to your pain and that your worship of God will finally be simply cold and dutiful. You fear that the faint flicker of love that now only slightly warms your heart will eventually be snuffed out by the cruel caretaker of your soul.

Sometimes when I am trapped inside that cage—when my soul is imprisoned—I find myself slipping to the conclusion that Michelle reached: Perhaps the soul is eternally damned, perhaps there is no just or loving God who cares about the soul—just a God. In such moments I am seized by the panicky thought that the only way to stifle the pain of my tormented soul is to live this life as an animal.

Tell the lies, play the game, get what you are after, don't expect respect and don't give it. Despise the people to whom you sell your body, and laugh the whole way to hell.

Fortunately, I have always been mercifully rescued from that abyss. And if you are reading this book and understand the pain, then thankfully somehow you too have been rescued.

We are not alone.

It is frightening to have encountered pain so extreme that we would sell our soul to escape its ravages. This is when we must fight. We must insist that no one will raid our inner sanctum and take what belongs only to us. The ultimate victory for those who would abuse us would be the defeat of our dignity, the dispossession of our souls.

There is no easy way through this struggle. It is, in the final analysis, the substance of all life's skirmishes. It's at the heart of our existence every morning as we get out of bed. Yes, we can accurately say that all battles eventually lead to the doorstep of our soul.

So fight. Fight mostly because in the darkness, when nothing else makes sense, you at least love yourself enough to resist the one who would rip your heart to pieces.

And fight because we have one who has gone before us. He was murdered by the religious club of his day, those pious, self-righteous leaders who plundered the souls of those who came seeking shelter in the sanctuary. Jesus comes to our side with the honorable distinction of having been booted by the religious establishment. He wrestles for the rescue of our soul while they try to make us twice the sons and daughters of hell they are.

Go figure.

3

The Religion of Our Cage

Jesus just wouldn't be tamed.

He insisted on breaking sabbath rules, he called the leading pastor-teachers of his day "whitewashed tombstones," and when he disagreed with the way the religious establishment was being run, he did not draft a proposal of suggested changes for the elders' consideration; he grabbed a whip instead.

And he endangered his donor base by hanging around prostitutes, drunkards, and robbers. The head of his public relations firm, John the Baptist, didn't have enough sense to be diplomatic with the local mayor. "It's wrong to have sex with your brother's wife," John told him, and he literally lost his head over it.

Jesus did not fit in well with the Religious Businessmen's Fellowship either. He told them it was impossible to serve both God and money, that it is almost out of the question for a rich man to get into heaven (unless you give it all away—but then what does that make you?), and that a widow giving a mere mite at the temple door was giving more than these wealthy buzzards even though they emptied bags of gold into the synagogue coffers. That fellow just could not be bought.

Even his career counseling program didn't measure up to approved, responsible guidelines. He never preached on the seven steps to vocational fulfillment. He told his followers they would have to deny themselves, take up their crosses (their *what?*), and live for others. And they were not to worry about future financial stability: If they were faithful with the talents God gave them, multiplying the reach of the kingdom, their personal needs would be met by the one who owns all the cattle in Texas and more.

Oh, and you fellows who are campaigning for a Reconstructed Roman Empire where Caesar bows to Yahweh: Love your enemies. And when they hack your body in two, throw your brittle frame to the lions for afternoon sport, and torch your flesh for evening lights, pray with all your heart that their souls will be saved.

This same unorthodox, first-century Jesus is on the loose today.

Sure you'll find him in Sunday school classes, pulpits, seminaries, and seminars, but you'll also find him in situations that seem out of control, unpredictable, and in bad taste. We just can't seem to manage his extravagant tendency to circumvent our time-honored ways of being good Christians.

You'll find his kingdom thriving in atheistic countries, spreading like wildfire. No matter that an oppressive, godless regime there stifles religion and personal rights; their Jesus—one like the New Testament Savior—is more powerful than any government's pathetic designs on the human soul. There his kingdom grows at a pace that outstrips anything the militarily strong and free "God-fearing" West has ever seen. The same can be said for Latin countries, where poverty and revolution cannot seem to quell the fire of pentecostals in love with their Messiah.

He can be found in contemporary mission structures that, by conventional standards, are poorly managed. Thousands join their ranks with revolutionary ideals of love and justice. Most of these volunteers haven't been to seminary, and some can't even spell the word "doctrinal." They don't know that Sunday is different from any other day of the week. But they can pray for hours, love their neighbors into the kingdom, forgo their "God-given" American rights, move five times in as many years, and trust God for miraculous interventions that, most of us are taught, were meant for some other dispensation.

On weeknights you'll find Jesus in local bars comforting bankrupt businesspersons, depressed blue-collar workers, lonely spouses, and disillusioned teenagers.

On Saturday nights you'll find him in parties and dance clubs, mixing with people who are "sick" but can't find the Doctor. They've been told he's in a church, but every time they knock on the door someone throws them a policy manual with all sorts of requirements and limitations. Some kind of hospital.

Look for him in refugee camps where responsible Christians don't go because of the chances of contracting disease, or look for him in hospices where AIDS patients lie dying and rejected by people who are expert in casting the first stone. See, he's in the inner city, where his car was stolen last week and where rain leaks through his apartment roof.

Yes, Jesus is in weird places doing some pretty wild stuff, and the darndest thing is, he's not asking our permission.

But what the heck? He's winning millions to himself, feeding scores of hungry people, reuniting broken families, healing cripples, alcoholics, and the mentally depressed. Prostitutes, homosexuals, welfare recipients, and communists are feeling the warmth of his love, and career-oriented, culture-bound Christians are being set free.

Hallelujah!

Unless, of course, he broke the rules.

What's the point I'm making? Back to Palestine. How is it possible that those who made it their profession to direct others toward God could not recognize him when he walked into their synagogue service? That's exactly what happened. This is not so much a harsh indictment of the Pharisees as it is a warning to us. Probably no other group of people has taken as much care as did these religious leaders to create laws, safeguards, that would protect both the purity of faith and the way to Yahweh. But Jesus didn't come as they expected, and in the name of God they killed God. What makes us think we are any different?

The Pharisees had created a system to aid them in their pursuit of God, and unfortunately the system itself took on religious significance. Their regimen of priestly activity became their measure of commitment and affirmed in their minds that all was well between them and their Creator. Discipline has a way of instilling a smug, haughty sense of self. Worse, it can insulate us from the nudges of the Spirit that would woo us away from our religious activity into a living and dynamic relationship with our Lord.

Jesus was explicit in his inaugural speech that he was going to hang around the brokenhearted, abused, imprisoned, orphaned, the widowed and the hungry. That is how the Old Testament foretold him, and that is how he lived.

The Pharisees, on the other hand, felt that his lifestyle validated their case that he was sent from hell. Look at him, a party animal who hangs around the drunks, bums, and cheats. In one of Jesus' confrontations with the Pharisees he told them that in the rigid practice of their religion—the observing of tithes and sabbaths— they had forgotten the "weightier matters of the law," which are to do justice and to love mercy. These learned keepers of the sanctuary knew by heart the parallel passages in the Prophets from which Jesus drew these injunctions. Here Israel was told that the Lord required justice and mercy and that true fasting was not measured by the rules of tithing and such but rather by the treatment of the hungry and the oppressed.

Church life today is much the same as it was for the Pharisees back then—a systematized attempt to follow the ways of God. We will never understand Jesus as long as we measure him against our structures. Rather, our structures need to undergo a certain ruthless measuring against Jesus. The process can be threatening, but it might also save our souls.

Jesus warns the church in Matthew 25 that we are subject to the same dangers as the Pharisees, that it is possible to live our entire lives with him as our religious "Lord" but not actually our Lord: I was hungry and you gave me nothing to eat, I was thirsty and you gave me nothing to drink, I was a stranger and you did not invite me in, I needed clothes and you did not clothe me, I was sick and in prison and you did not look after me. Depart from me into eternal darkness.

Salvation does not come by works. Neither is it assured by religion. Wise men and women would want to hesitate just a tad after reading these words of Jesus.

So, now to the point: We are oppressed by tortuous pain, and we have decided to fight for our souls. But to fight for our souls, we must first be freed from religion.

Religion is a parasite that can live only if it is attached to structures that harbor souls, because souls are its food. And the devastating fact is that "church" all too often sets the banquet table. The disastrous implications of that fact are not some distant possibility, they are upon us today.

It is religion that seduced the German church to exchange its soul for the pride of race. A haughty elevation of heritage, of having birthed Luther and the Reformation, Beethoven and Bach, blinded Christians to the demonic presence in their structures and pushed them far from God during Germany's desperate hour. (Understand that the Pharisees carried with them the baggage of being God's chosen people—what a heady heritage, what a haven for puffed-up souls ready to crucify the very one who designated them chosen!) A scant minority of church leaders resisted Hitler's designs on Germany; the vocal majority of church leaders chastised Martin Niemöller, Dietrich Bonhoeffer, and friends who adamantly opposed racist, nationalistic visions as contradicting love's call to esteem others more highly than ourselves.

Six million Jews: children, women, men. Killed by religion, served to the ovens by the church.

South Africa's earth holds half the world's gold and more than two-thirds of the world's diamonds. This little country the size of California has enough wealth to lavish comfort on all its citizens, yet every year more than 200,000 black children die of starvation. There is only one doctor for every 19,000 blacks, half the blacks are unemployed, and hundreds of thousands of black men are forced to live separate from their families for the greater part of each year to work in white-owned industries.

In South Africa there is a saying: "If you feed the hungry they call you a Christian. If you ask why they are hungry they call you a communist."

Why should it be so threatening to understand the causes of hunger? Because the closer you get to its roots, the more chilling the picture of a state church that not only created the system of apartheid but for decades also provided the ongoing moral basis to keep it alive. As in Nazi Germany, in South Africa it is the church that crusades for the vision of an all-white nation to be formed, if necessary, at the cost of human life. Those disposable Jews and blacks.

No amount of political reasoning or anthropological gymnastics can justify the human carnage. Our insidious twisting of truth in the attempts to defend such systems all too clearly illustrates the degree to which religion is eating our souls alive.

And what of our own nation's high view of its history and "divine" destiny? Are we any different from this century's Germany and South Africa? Do we, the white subsection, exhibit a pride of race and heritage that blinds us to the racism and classism that mark our sanctuaries on Sundays?

I spoke with the pastor who kicked the prostitute Michelle out of his sanctuary. He seemed to believe that he had done God a favor by keeping the temple holy. Truth is, his sanctuary was no more holy than the nightclub where Michelle sold her body. At least Michelle was honest about her condition. Not so with the sanctuary—there the good Christians strutted about like the fellow who raised his hands to God in thanksgiving that he was "not like other men robbers, evildoers, adulterers." Jesus tells us that meanwhile a man stood downcast in the corner of the temple and pleaded with God to be merciful to him. We know from the story who went away forgiven.

It is critical that in your time of pain and healing you know that Jesus never succumbed to religion. More than that, he despised it. "Woe to you, teachers of the law and Pharisees, you hypocrites! You shut the kingdom of heaven in men's faces. You yourselves do not enter, nor will you let those enter who are trying to" (Matthew 23:13).

Welcome to the wild and dangerous life of Jesus. There are very few rules, and there certainly is no religion. Scream. Laugh. Romp. Cry. Party till you rouse the entire town, and then party some more. Drink his wine to the very last, and dance till you drop with the exhaustion of a spirit set free.

And then fight. Fight and fight and continue to fight, because you're no child of religion.

4

Charlatan Saviors

You've got a lot of nerve to say you are my friend
—Bob Dylan

All sorts of people are ready to save our soul—not least among them being those who would plunder it. Being set free from religion is a process that unfolds to us as we contemplate the saviors who have supposedly come to our rescue. All of them pose as our friends, and few of them will settle for anything less than submission and servitude.

Absolute freedom maddens them.

Salvation is what religion offers, and it comes in the most innocuous forms: mission programs, denominations, Christian colleges, doctrinal creeds, baptisms, governments, political agendas, and rules stipulating proper moral conduct. They manage to win our allegiance through the promise of drawing us closer to God and relieve us of our fear that we are not measuring up to God's standards. And, of course, religion replaces that fear with the fear of failing to follow its own prescribed route to pleasing God.

You see, religion socializes us. By that I mean it puts us into a group of people where now we belong. We are family, we have identity, we are accepted. I follow the rules and they approve of me. (The group may say they "love" me.) I break the rules and they chastise me (for my own good, of course). This process is not unique to religion; it is the most basic description of how society operates. We become so dependent on the group, which has now become our reference point for what is right and wrong, that our very self becomes a reflection of the group's values and beliefs. In fact, our self-worth is measured by our perception of what the group thinks of us. Madison Avenue has developed the art of arousing that sense at the cash register: The cars, clothes, houses, and furniture we own say who we are in relation to other people. We are discriminating customers—both in whom we are like and in whom we are not like. Take away the need for others' approval and Madison Avenue would crash.

The process of socialization, then, is the means whereby we learn the rules of the "in club" and then adjust our lives accordingly. This is how we win their affections. Not that this is a highly conscious process—we are much more aware of how teenagers are victim to this process than of how we ourselves are.

Religion's socialization process is lethal. It not only offers us the acceptance and affections of a specific group of people, it also offers us the acceptance and affection of God. We become secure in our religious sense of self and vigorously join with the others in defending the fundamentals of our worldview. This is what much of our Christian education is about. A judicious understanding of our fallenness would allow the perspective that a certain percentage of Sunday school classes, sermons, doctrine courses, and seminars are not as much about pursuit of truth as they are about religious socialization.

It's no accident, incidentally, that churches are quite easily characterized along socioeconomic lines. This is a black church from a poor neighborhood, over there is an all-white church from the suburbs, and just a block away is a yuppie church that is not distinguished so much by its ethnicity as it is by its high percentage of aerospace engineers. Theological seminaries offer courses that ensure the perpetuation of religious socialization: Classes are given on the so-called church growth principles, predicated on the idea that the best way to expand is to associate with people who are like yourself. They call it the "homogeneous principle," and in fact it is nothing more than spiritualized racism and classism.

The acceptance and affection of God offered to us by religious socialization come with high stakes. Any rejection of this religious group's values and behavioral expectations will bring down upon us the wrath and rejection of not only the group but also God.

To become free people is to unleash the indignation of religion.

We must be clear that the journey to freedom is at times a bleak and lonely path, one that offers us few of the familiar comforts that came with religion. We are left to ourselves to discover our true salvation, and we are often confronted by the animosity of those who find our freedom a threat to their religious tranquillity.

In these situations we face the challenge of our will—do we want freedom badly enough to endure the ambiguities, marginalization, and misunderstandings that will come with our apparent obstinacy and betrayal of what we have been taught? These discomforts certainly will be our partners along the way.

Ambiguity, because the life of freedom will be uncharted for us. Where once there was mostly just black and white, we will find that much has turned gray. A simple example of this is the moral trauma of a teenager who was reared to believe that movies are of the devil. Now he or she is attending a Christian college where moviegoing has no more of a moral implication than taking a shower. Consequently, the student eventually tags along with some peers to see something as harmless as *Superman II* but squirms through the entire screening because of the uncomfortable feeling that he or she is sinning. Our flight to freedom—away from religion—will constantly put us into conflict with our particular moral upbringing.

There's no road map here, simply an uneasy, unschooled conscience that has to meet Jesus anew.

And we will experience *marginalization*, because the religious system must label us as somewhat heretical if it is to ensure that its other subjects do not interpret our deviance as a legitimate option.

Fear combined with negative labels has a powerful effect. If I have been trained to believe that a "liberal" is one who has rejected Jesus personally, then I certainly do not want to be one of them and face the consequences of eternal separation in hell. I am likely to avoid certain behaviors or opinions if I have been convinced that they reflect a liberal orientation. Those in our group who have trespassed the boundaries will be put aside, partly in the hope that their isolation will lead to repentance, and partly because we are implementing the biblical injunction to "expel the immoral one" from our midst. And if we are honest with ourselves, we will admit that we avoid personal contact with them because we also fear their impact on our own minds and souls.

I used to attend a church that expelled a young woman from the congregation because she had had an experience of the Holy Spirit that in her opinion led to speaking in tongues. That church's doctrinal statement did not allow for this particular interpretation of Scripture, and they tried to convince her to renounce the experience. She refused, and one Sunday she was "disfellowshipped" in front of the entire congregation. Church members were instructed to treat her as an "unbeliever" until she came back to the Lord (read: back to their doctrinal statement). A spiritual battle had been won, and the congregation felt all the more secure in its practice of religion.

"Give me that old-time religion 'cause it's good enough for me!"

Misunderstandings will also be a part of our experience in the flight from religion. We'll blunder countless times with our newfound freedom as we attempt to articulate our contempt for the chains of our past. The conflicts that we are sure to engage will regularly be our own doing. But because we are freshly enrolled students, we must allow that it takes several rounds of learning to navigate our new course in the subcultures of religion. We will hurt and offend others as we describe our encounters with Christ, because they will interpret our experience as a judgment of their own values and practices. This is not easily avoided and in fact is sometimes necessary, because at times the gospel is offensive.

An African-American friend of mine, who is a prominent evangelical leader, recently attended a national conference on the United States' religious heritage. Plenary speakers predictably extolled the establishment of America as an act of God to spread light to all the nations. Current national ills coupled with the rise of "secular humanism" were decried as the great enemies of the country as established by the Founding Fathers, and prayers were offered up to God, with much passion, begging for a return to the good old days. Amens resounded throughout the assembly hall. My friend walked over to the microphone and prayed this simple prayer: "Dear God, please don't ever let us return to the good old days—I don't think us black folk could survive them." With that he sat down.

You can imagine the number of people who communicated their offense at his having stifled the blessed move of the Spirit during that plenary session. Religion blinded these white evangelical leaders to the truth of their national heritage. My friend's statement was offensive simply because the gospel is narrow-minded on the subject of racism. No, God will not bless our request to go back to the days when blacks were not received as children of God, unable to bear the same dignity as whites—that would be blasphemy against God's creative masterpiece called the human race.

Our experience of religion has hurt us, and it is our great fortune that in the middle of all the pain we have stumbled into the glorious freedom of Jesus Christ. This is perhaps the most refreshing and rejuvenating encounter available to the Christian. We had accepted the burdens and chains of religion as being a part of our salvation, but now we are free simply to love Jesus with all our hearts and to love our neighbors as ourselves. Good-bye to the rules and regulations that would make us prisoners in others' sanctuaries. The Pharisees hated Jesus for this freedom, and in the most vulnerable description of God ever recorded we find Jesus pleading, "My soul is overwhelmed with sorrow to the point of death. . . . if it is at all possible, may this cup be taken from me." He was hours away from being murdered by a coalition of the religious establishment and the government.

If we insist on fighting for our freedom, which I pray to God we will, then we must know that we are choosing to enter into a battle that will rage against our being. We cannot be surprised at the wounds.

There is yet a more crushing discovery in our journey to freedom: the realization that people or institutions that we had regarded as precious friends were actually charlatans. They invited us to trust them with our most vulnerable self, our soul, and we gave it to them. In truth, they had no legitimate basis to offer us what only God can deliver. And similarly, there are those whom we had regarded as precious friends who turned against us because we no longer held to the regulations of their religious club. It had been in our hearts that the friendship was no token of mutual club membership, but rather a genuine encounter of tenderness, care, and trust.

Loneliness and betrayal are experienced in their most acute forms under these circumstances. There is a darkness, a desperate void. This is a place of abandonment, where words that describe pain cannot probe deep enough to give meaning to our hell.

Vicious gashes inflicted by the enemy of our soul—yes, that fits our concept of the utterly contemptible deeds of evil. But who has words to give voice to the grief of a soul's friends-turned-foes? Whether their offerings were a sincere gesture or a sinister ploy is not of initial concern to us as we begin to taste our pain. We are undone.

We must grasp that we are ultimately and continually abandoned by those who would save us, because in fact they are not able to save us. Their inability to deliver is simple reality.

And neither can we save ourselves.

Stripped-down, naked, and crucified Jesus. This is my only consolation during the despairing times. I'm not talking about the doctrinal Jesus whom some religious charlatans propagate: the one who offers an idea of salvation that relates basically if not exclusively to the eternal resting place of our souls. This is not at all to question the absolute necessity for the forgiveness of our sins through the atoning death of Jesus Christ. No, we rigorously defend and affirm that truth. But to relegate salvation simply to the category of eternal security is to belittle the incarnation of God— and it denies us the privilege of Christ's forceful and compassionate intervention in the tangled mess of our daily lives.

I am always desperately in need of Jesus.

Sometimes I go to look for him in a cathedral. There, in an off-hour when I have the entire sanctuary to myself, I will choose the back pew and still my racing heart. The stained-glass windows on either side of me direct my focus down the center aisle and up the wall till I rest my gaze in the compelling reach of Jesus' eyes. There we are, just the two of us. Sometimes for an hour or more. Simple Jesus, uncluttered by religion. He understands my pain. He hangs there pitifully, empathically, convincingly.

Finally I am able to pour out to him what he already knows, and I weep the pain as my mind screams its ruin. And ornate windows flicker from the lighted wick of a soul about to be snuffed out. Then I hear it, "My *God*, my *God,* why have you forsaken me?" It is Jesus, doubled over from the vile and cruel rejection, that prison of the soul. He knows. Then he reaches for my shoulders with his bloody hands, and we swing about the sanctuary in the dance of pain. The place of tenderness is enlarged. The shrieking, the howling, and the laughter. Eventually, we lie prostrate on the floor in the exhaustion of honesty and torment, the all-encompassing, peaceful embrace of fellowship in suffering.

Yes, he knows.

Then this orphan of religion shuts the sanctuary door behind him and sets his face toward home. I am free, delightfully and outrageously free. And hell itself writhes with pain as the heel smashes into the temple of the serpent's head.

5

Hold On to Your Soul

Freedom of the soul can cost our lives.

As a child I remember wishing I could have lived in the days of Jesus' sojourn on earth. It would have been much easier, I thought, to believe in and follow Christ if I had touched his hands, watched him perform miracles, and listened to his wisdom without the interruption of two thousand years' worth of hand-me-down writings.

Of course I never really thought too much about the cost of being a Christian in those early days. So much of the teaching that circulated in early church correspondence (the letters of the New Testament) discussed the natural connection between hardship and following Jesus. It was not in the small print at the bottom of the contract; rather, it was the bold type at the top: "Don't be surprised at the suffering," "Endure hardship as a good soldier," "When they drag you into court. . . ." In fact, eleven of Jesus' specially selected disciples were martyred for their faith.

Persecution was no academic subject back then. The question was more along the line of wondering if God would be able to sustain the follower during the time of trial. After the burning of Rome in A.D. 64, Christians were singled out as scapegoats by both the Roman rulers and the Jewish religious leaders. The art of torture was perfected.

Christians were subjected to elaborate torture whose goal was not the death of the body but rather capitulation to the emperor. To claim Jesus as Lord in the face of the emperor was to deny the Roman sovereign's dominion and right to one's soul. One form of torture was an iron grid that was heated up over a fire. The Christian was thrown naked on the grid and flopped about to escape the pain but of course could not get off until allowed. He was taken back to the prison cell for recovery; then, when the wounds were close to healed, he was once again transported to the red-hot grill. The opportunity was given to proclaim Caesar as lord. If he declined, the prisoner would be thrown on the grid for another round of frying, after which he was escorted back to the cell and held for the next searing session. The hope of the emperor was that pain, fatigue, and infections would eventually wear out the Christian spirit. It was a contest of the souls.

Christians dubbed this prison experience "going on retreat." Through it the senses were cleared and the true priorities of following Christ distilled. Quite different from our retreats into the Rocky Mountains. It was a given to these Christians that freedom of the soul could lead to death, and they loved their souls enough to choose freedom.

Ivo Lesbaupin's book *Blessed Are the Persecuted* is a chilling record of those early days. In it he describes the choice facing imprisoned Christians:

> Deprived of material goods and comforts, having to bear the stench, the promiscuity, the unspeakably bad food, the cold, hunger, thirst, isolation, the dark, fetters, and all of the rest, Christians in prison had to discover their source of life, gladness, and communion within themselves. This source was faith. In the absence of all material or sensible support and comfort, faith became stronger, firmer. Christians were no longer dissipated by the innumerable compensations of the life of the free. They were led to delve for the essential, they had to find the raison d'être of their lives, their struggle, their hope

in God alone. Now they came to appreciate true freedom, a freedom independent of walls and iron bars, a liberty within them. It was their decision whether to lose it or develop it.

Choosing the freedom of our souls. . . .

History has served up this choice to Christians countless times, and for reasons that no doubt are strange to our modern ears. Here are just a few examples. John Wycliffe preached in the 1300s that God is our sole and ultimate authority. He claimed that faith in Jesus is all that is necessary for salvation. The bishop of London censured him for that view and forbade him to preach, even though he was a parish priest. Wycliffe, excluded from public life because of his choice to hold to the freedom of his soul, retired to his office, and there he translated the entire Bible into the world's first English edition. Possession of an English-language Bible was illegal (in England!), and Wycliffe's work was banned. After his death in 1384, a formal hearing ordered all of his writings burned, and in 1428 Wycliffe's body was exhumed and then burned as a heretic's.

John Hus, a late contemporary of Wycliffe, spread his teachings in Bohemia, where he drew a large following. Faith in Jesus did not require subservience to the church, he preached. Hus was excommunicated and taken to trial. The church found him guilty and told him to recant or face burning at the stake. Hus was a free man, and he paid the price. Tradition tells us that as the flames licked about his body with the church leaders looking on, Hus sang praises to God. This practice of praising Jesus while on fire was followed by others who subsequently faced the same fate. Eventually, the church, chagrined by its inability to gain submission even in death, silenced future martyrs with wood screws driven into their tongues before they were led publicly to the stake.

Two hundred years later, Quaker Mary Fisher was holding theological conversations with students at Cambridge University. By this time the Bible was legally available in English, and in the very country where earlier men had been killed for their possession of such, now they openly studied it. But women were not so fortunate. Spiritual insight belonged only to men. Mary Fisher broke the law by having theological discussions with male students. As punishment, the mayor of the town had her stripped naked to the waist and then flogged publicly.

Elizabeth Hooten, a seventy-year-old Quaker missionary, set sail from England to Massachusetts to do evangelistic work. When she attempted to settle there and buy property, the Puritan leaders tied her to a cart and transported her through several New England towns, where, each time, the elderly woman was stripped to the waist and then flogged. Finally they tied her to a horse, took her far into the mountains, and there abandoned her to the wild animals. Hooten knew that men's cruelty could not silence her soul. She survived the ordeal and set sail for Jamaica, where she continued to serve as a missionary until her death.

Early Christians were persecuted by the Jewish leaders and secular government of the day. Wycliffe, Hus, Fisher, Hooten, and hundreds of thousands of Christians since have been persecuted by the church. To be sure, all of them could have avoided the hardship by succumbing to the demands of the religious leadership, but they chose freedom for their souls instead.

Of course all the torture was done in the name of defending the purity of the faith. Religious socialization is expert and ruthless in the pursuit of its ends.

Nico Smith's story clearly illustrates the effectiveness of religious socialization in society today. Having been carefully reared to be a good white Afrikaner, he grew in public stature till he served as one of South Africa's most prominent theologians at Stellenbosch University—the training ground for most of South Africa's Afrikaans preachers. There the twisted rationales for apartheid were justified with the Scripture, and students graduated without ever having been challenged to change the way their church-run society treated blacks. Like all Afrikaner leaders in good standing, Nico was a member of the Broederbond, the secret white society sworn to the goal of creating an all-white South Africa.

Nico told me about his socialization process: "I can still remember one of my earliest impressions was of my mother telling me that you just don't talk to a black person unless you want to give him an order.

"As in most Afrikaner houses, blacks working in our home had a separate tin plate and tin utensils. In our house those were put on a shelf deep down in one of the kitchen cupboards. Sometimes, I remember, while we were playing around as kids, crawling into one of the shelves, I accidentally touched those plates. A sibling would run to my mother and say, 'Niki touched those plates and cups!' My mother would tell me, 'Go wash your hands immediately! Don't go near there.'"

The first time Nico was confronted with the possibility of eating with blacks was after he had completed his theological studies and served five years in the pastorate. He went to a conference at a German-run mission base, and lunch was set for all attending, including some black pastors and evangelists.

"I couldn't sit down. I had a psychological block," Nico said. The missionary's wife had to lay a separate table for Nico in the study. "I sat there all by myself, having my meal all alone."

Nico was convinced that these missionaries just didn't know any better. This sort of social mixing could lead to mixed marriages, "at which point you lose your identity, your God-given identity," according to all that Nico had been taught. Back then he thought that one had to protect the purity of race— this was a moral, religious duty. It was obvious to Nico that these missionaries did not understand what blacks really were.

Sure as he was about his views of white superiority, doubts began to arise because he realized that these were fellow black Christians.

When Nico was in his late forties he visited a black township for the first time. Disease, death, malnutrition, unsanitary conditions, and overcrowding made for a squalor he could never have imagined. Shocked by the suffering he encountered, Nico began to wonder if the God of Abraham really meant for blacks to live in such dehumanizing conditions.

Few whites in South Africa—under one percent—have ever been to a black township. In fact, that is the genius of apartheid: It keeps blacks and whites in two separate worlds. Religious socialization can work unhindered. A tourist or visiting evangelist can spend a week in South Africa and think that the country is the same thriving, prosperous land Nico knew before he allowed himself to see the conditions of blacks as they actually were.

The physical layout of the black regions protects innocent white eyes from witnessing the true plight of blacks. Black townships are hidden in the hills; the highways that take white commuters from their suburban homes to the major cities do not pass through places like Soweto. As long as they live normal white lives and stay on main roads—heeding the government propaganda that warns about the unpredictable, dangerous nature of blacks—ordinary citizens, and even sincere, mature Christians, never know the hurts their lifestyles inflict on blacks. Such separation is critical for religious socialization.

When Nico first saw this reality, he had to go back to his Bible and ask some tough questions. In 1963, he had traveled to Europe and met Karl Barth, one of Protestantism's leading theologians, who had also led one of the resistance movements against Hitler's racist ambitions for Germany.

At the end of their conversation, Barth startled Nico by asking him whether he felt free to preach the gospel in South Africa. Nico recounted their conversation to me.

"Barth asked me, 'Do you feel free to say whatever the gospel may tell you to say?'

"I said, 'Yes, I think I'm free.' At the time I really thought I was.

"'It is not that easy just to say yes,' Barth responded. 'Will you be willing to preach the gospel if you are convinced that the gospel is saying things your friends and community wouldn't like you to preach?'

"'I don't experience it that way,' I told him. 'I don't know how I'll react if I get in that situation.'

"'It's even more serious than that,' Barth cautioned. 'Will you be willing to proclaim the gospel if the government in your country says you may not proclaim that understanding of the gospel?'

"'I can't think that the government in my country would ever do a thing like that,' I responded."

Returning to South Africa, Nico slowly began to see that the government and church succeeded in winning his soul in exchange for the benefits of wealth, comfort, and feelings of racial superiority. He was a fully socialized Christian white.

As Nico explored his new understanding, his preaching began to change. Predictably, he was called before the deacons, and after several unsuccessful attempts to reorient his mind back to the club's view of the straight and narrow, Nico was defrocked from the Dutch Reformed Church—the denomination to which most Afrikaners belong. The right to preach was granted only to those who believed in the Afrikaner dream.

Nico resigned from the secret white-supremacy society, the Broederbond. "I really got liberated," Nico told me. "I really began to preach the gospel." He left one of the most prestigious positions a person can hold in South Africa, that of a university professor, and accepted the call to pastor a small black church, where he has since served with humility and commitment.

The price has been high. Nico and his wife Ellen not only lost their position of prestige among the religious and political leaders of the nation but also were labeled "liberals," "nigger-lovers," "communists," and "unpatriotic." Worse, family members shunned them for bringing "shame" to the faith, clan, and country.

Religion found the white South African church a fertile place to breed souls for food. And as in Hitler's Germany, it married the Scriptures to its political agenda and won the allegiance of millions who were duped into fervently defending the brutal system of apartheid out of faithfulness to God. I have stood through countless ceremonies in South Africa in which whites have sung the national anthem, said the pledge of allegiance, and then closed with what is de facto the national Afrikaner hymn:

> O God, our help in ages past
> Our hope for years to come
> Our shelter from the stormy blast
> And our eternal home.

It is astonishing to realize that South Africa's religious socialization has been effective in reaching many American whites. Famous white TV evangelists and super-preachers continue to court

South Africa's state president and parliament and label the black liberation movement as communist or socialist-inspired. I have interviewed dozens of American missionaries serving there who scoff at the notion of turning their century-old labors over to black Christian leaders. In their view, the blacks are incapable of running ministry as well as whites can. Besides being blatantly racist, these pronouncements conceal a deeper issue: the fear that black-led ministries would no doubt interrupt the process of white religious socialization, which justifies the power white missionaries exercise over black nationals, and would introduce ideas that affirm the dignity of blacks, not just whites. Whites rightly perceive that blacks would alter some of the theology and structures that have been maintained and propagated by the powerful.

When we gave our hearts to Jesus, the "untrained" and natural response of our new God-given characters was to treat all men and women with dignity. We had no way of knowing that Christianity, as a system, is so intertwined with the world's systems that it often calls us to allegiance to structures and traditions that squash the dignity of others.

Perhaps you live in a cage of pain that is largely the result of being chastised for following this natural instinct of the Holy Spirit. You are getting the message that in order to be accepted by the religious club you have to put aside those sensibilities—you are being encouraged to trade in your soul for the club's love and affection.

Don't do it.

I continually meet young Christians in the United States who have been labeled and mistreated by the church for not being "good Christians" (more honestly, for not holding to the religious system's particular political agenda). They have been shunned by their home church, cut from the missionary budget, relieved of their teaching posts in Sunday school and at Christian colleges, dropped from reference boards, and kicked out of evangelistic organizations. One was pulled from a conference program at the last minute even though his talk had been widely publicized: Certain major donors had threatened to withdraw finances because they did not agree with that speaker's political views. Women have been removed from their preaching slots at missionary conventions because large, conservative donor churches threatened to boycott the events. An evangelical publishing house destroyed thousands of copies of already-printed books because donors to its nonprofit parent corporation warned that they would withdraw support due to publications that were too critical of legalistic tendencies in the church.

There is no courage, tolerance, teachability, or humility shown by those who are governed by religion.

The way of discipleship is not easy. As we are changed more and more into the image of Christ, we will encounter the opposition of religion. Our desire to be faithful to the Scripture will lead to confrontation.

Once again, we are faced with the painful realization that we have been betrayed. Too often we will come to understand that many of the friends, church groups, and family members who seemed to be wonderfully close in spirit are actually keepers of the religious door, and that we have their love and support only to the degree that we cling to their religious, political, and economic ideology. We will ache with the loss of love.

We are orphans, we are homeless, we are the enemy.

This pain will tempt us to let go of our spiritual sensitivities in exchange for comfort, but we must say no. We must resist to the point of stifling loneliness and wait for our way of escape. Hold on to your soul. Hold on to those things that give life to your soul. They are your lifejackets, if you will, at a time like this. Swim the sea of your distress, and don't sacrifice yourself to the first life raft that comes your way promising relief.

We must insist that to be Christian does not mean we have to be racist, sexist, bigoted, ethnocentric, and classist. We must have courage to venture into new structures, abandoning old ones if they insist on silencing our souls. Some of us will even have to let go of structures we ourselves created.

The simple fact is that we are new people. What we have learned and experienced has changed us. Whereas we used to sing, "This world is not my home, I'm just a-passin' through," and thought we were describing a pure life totally detached from the ways of the world, now we wonder if in fact we were living totally attached to the evil systems of this world and if, possibly, we were riding a train whose destination was hell.

Jesus beckons us to leave that world and follow him. And as Bonhoeffer wrote before being hung with piano wire by Nazi guards for resisting Hitler's crusade, "When Jesus bids a man come, he bids him come and die."

We are not alone. The Scriptures say that we are surrounded by a great cloud of witnesses who have gone before. The author of Hebrews tells us some faced jeers and flogging, while other were chained and put in prison. They were stoned, they were sawed in two, they were put to death by the sword. They went about in sheepskins and goatskins, destitute, persecuted, and mistreated. They wandered in deserts and mountains and in caves and holes in the ground.

They have received a final home where there is no crying or pain or rejection. Only the pure, undefiled love of Jesus.

So let's persevere in the face of rape, dishonor, labeling, disfellowship, confusion, and loneliness. We are those who do not shrink back, because our hearts are filled with the warmth of one who went to hell and back to buy us our freedom.

Yes, we are alive, we are free. We are a sorry-looking sight: bedraggled, crippled, defiled, and broken. We are outcasts, but we are totally liberated outcasts. We have learned what religious lords consider the most frightening fact of all: You can kill the body but you cannot kill the soul.

Hold on to your soul.

PART TWO

Identify the Bars

Envision Your Freedom
Devastation
Disapproval
Disappointment
Distance
Spiritual Codependency
Bitterness
Cynicism
Disillusionment
Our Own Bumbling

6

Envision Your Freedom

We are new people and will need to learn to live as new people. All sorts of emotions will dominate us, and at times we may even panic at their intensity.

Have we gone crazy? Are we lost? Perhaps what others have said about us is true.

We have changed, and because of that our world is jumbled. We are disoriented. It is no longer the neat and tidy package that had more answers than questions. Whereas Sunday hymns and sermons used to bring us comfort, now they nauseate us. Whereas we used to respect certain Christian leaders and groups, now we find them reprehensible. We are surprised by our vehement pronouncements against others, and we're besieged all the more by doubt.

Where once we experienced peace, now there is conflict; fellowship, now broken relationships; release, now bondage; uplifting, now oppression.

Listlessness and lack of goals haunt us where before we were visionary, energetic Christians who were always ready and willing to do any task for others. We derived meaning from our labors; now they are a necessary burden.

Our journey away from religion will necessarily be dark and difficult, and initially we will find few supports along the way. The theological foundations and church traditions that earlier gave sense to our confusing and unstable existence are now a part of the confusion. No grid or system of living has yet replaced them. It is as though we went to bed one night in a houseboat tied to a Los Angeles pier, then awoke in the morning to discover ourselves loose from the mooring. We are adrift and have no reference points to help us return to land. Experimentation and searching have become our daily pursuit.

We are dogged by our negative experiences. We cannot put them behind us and return to "normal Christian living." If we only could, it would please those around us. To please them now, however, would be worse than having no moorings. We have enough self-respect to reject the normalcy and injury-to-the-soul the old club offers us.

Our inability to just snap out of it frustrates Christian friends and leaders, who postulate that if we would only trust God with more faith all would be well. They have no idea of our pain.

In the days ahead we will be facing certain decisions that all our church upbringing and training have taught us to avoid: A fundamentalist joins a wild charismatic congregation; a white woman reared in the suburbs moves into a poor ethnic neighborhood; a Baptist defects to an Episcopal fellowship, and vice versa; a woman divorces her husband; a child leaves his abusive parents.

As we face the barrage of new options and the doubts that naturally arise because of our religious socialization, we are afflicted with guilt. What was honestly an experience of Jesus and Christian fellowship? What was simply religious conditioning? Did the Truth actually set me free, or did I feel good because, after abiding by the group's truths, I received their affection and affirmation? There is no shortcut to answering these most serious and pressing questions. Our hurtful experiences make the very fundamentals of our faith suspect, and so we are unable to lean on traditional supports to make it through the painful recovery. Often, the deeper the pain, the more suspect our fundamentals. And so we're not only learning to live with the wounds but also forced out on a vulnerable quest for Truth.

We are also deluged by a whole set of emotions and feelings, such as hate and fear, that seem to control us. We cannot seem to put away the hurts inflicted on us, and we feel guilty for it. Why can't we just "forgive and forget"? Why not just write the whole thing off as a bad mistake or colossal misunderstanding? They were sincere when they inflicted pain on us, so why not just be a person of understanding—a good Christian—and let them off the hook? In fact, that would be a noble way to minister back to them.

A friend told me of his daily experience of carefully planning the demise of a fellow Christian who had hurt him. My friend would fantasize ways to threaten, torture, and otherwise abuse this man's wife and children while the man was tied to a chair and forced to watch. The longer and more vicious the pain inflicted on the family, the more satisfaction for my hurting friend.

"Am I alone?" he wondered about his horrible secret. No, he is not. If you have been terribly abused, then you too have probably imagined the demise of the one who violated your most private and tender parts. This normal reaction to pain is not an indication of who you are (a mean, unforgiving brute), but rather a measure of the violation you feel. The danger comes when we nurture these destructive notions and find ourselves at home with revenge. If mercy reaches us, we will eventually let go of the rage.

Healing takes time. We must know that after a while we inflict greater wounds on ourselves by nursing our hurts and replaying the tapes of revenge. If for no other reason than self-care, we must find motivation to put away the visions of dismembering our tormentors. It is as though they win a double victory against our soul if we allow our dreams of revenge and our uncontrollable rage to consume us. We must love ourselves enough to deny them that satisfaction. The daily reminder of their abuse only continues to inflict pain on our wounds and increase our agony.

And healing requires honesty. We cannot simply deny the pain and betrayal. Part of our process of becoming new and free people in-volves facing the wounds head-on—just as we would expect a doctor to deal directly with the physical wounds inflicted on us in a car accident. The gashes don't just go away. In fact, inattentiveness to a wound can lead to infection and more pain. How sorry the person who loses a leg to gangrene, when earlier focus on the wound could have resulted in healing. It hurts to relive the specifics of our painful encounters, but if we have the courage to do so, in time we will reap the healing.

And some of us will live with "ghost pains." People who have had a leg amputated report that they suffer excruciating pain in a toe or ankle that is actually no longer there. It is a very real, physical experience, and doctors are not able to make it go away. Are we to admonish, "Come on, fellow, leave the pain behind; you had the accident years ago"? Why should we expect that wounds to our souls will tarry any less? Like the amputee who must learn to live each day with the pain, so we may have to learn to thrive in life with the ever-present reminder of our misfortune and consequent pain. That will become our challenge.

Sometimes we need others to point out the wounds for us. It is possible that our pain is so intense that the source of our suffering is shielded from our conscious awareness. A friend who has gained our trust is able to lovingly point us to the source and free us to go through the difficult process of facing the real wound. If, for example, I have been hurt by someone very close to me, I may deny the source of pain because I cannot imagine living with the consequences of accepting betrayal. A solid friend can tenderly bring reality and cushioning to my life at the same moment. And a friend will be able to point out my own complicity in the betrayal that led to my pain. Few will be able to take this role, because pain lessens our trust of others. The depth of friendships is severely tested at these junctures.

In the next several chapters I have highlighted nine specific wounds that we may, to varying degrees, carry with us. As you read, focus on those that most accurately describe your encounter with pain. It's as though each of these were a bar on our prison window. We can take hold of them and deliberately begin to saw our way through. Simply identifying those bars has a liberating power in itself. Our freedom is in view.

As we honestly and courageously take charge of our lives by facing the pain, we will discover others who are walking down an almost identical path. We will find companionship in our afflictions, but more than that, we will provide each other with a human crutch as we hobble our way to health.

Maybe the prison guard will even have the presence of mind to laugh at the sight of several crippled escapees stumbling over each other's feet as they make their fumbling dash for freedom.

7

Devastation

It takes unusual commitment to move into a foreign culture, forgo the familiar comforts of showers, cars, TV, medical clinics, and English, and put several thousand miles between yourself and family. Larry and Jean's sense of God's call on their lives, to make these sacrifices in order to take the message of Jesus Christ to people who never had the opportunity to hear of his love, was compelling. "How can we selfishly enjoy the physical and familial benefits of the Western life while others suffer disease and face eternal separation from Jesus?" they asked themselves.

The adjustments were difficult as they went through the typical stages of culture shock, but they genuinely loved the people of their remote jungle village, and they persisted in the roughest of times because, as they used to remind themselves in those stressful moments, "the will of God will not lead you where the grace of God cannot keep you."

Tom, their unexpected late arrival, had been born on the mission field. Now his two siblings were back in the United States going through reverse culture shock and enjoying life in Christian college. These older two had paid the price of their parents' decision, leaving grade school friends and Saturday-morning cartoons, but there was little resentment as they reflected on the wealth of their international experience when compared to the more parochial upbringing of their college peers.

Jean was not able to ride the bumps of missionary living as easily as Larry, but she always managed to persevere in faith. Larry experienced the fulfillment of discipleship training, and Jean equally enjoyed supervising a health clinic.

Close to 9:30 one Thursday morning, Tom, now thirteen, was home in his bedroom—unknown to his parents. He heard his mom come into the kitchen and fumble about. Not sure what disturbed him about her fidgeting, Tom peeked through the crack between the door and the wall and froze at the sight.

Jean held a shotgun to her head, closed her eyes, and with a slow, deliberate movement splatted her brains all over the kitchen wall and ceiling. Larry, just outside, ran into the kitchen at the sound of gunfire. He knew it was Jean by the dress on the decapitated body. There were no missionary colleagues nearby to help as the stunned father and son cleaned Jean off the wall.

"It's simply unbelievable," Larry wrote me, "it's just unbelievable."

In a matter of seconds, the structure of his reality collapsed just as Jean's body had to the floor. Larry left the jungle with no road map to the future and no interpretation of the past. Life had turned into a senseless, unreferenced existence, and the love of his heart was reduced to maggots in a third-world hole in the ground.

The destruction of Larry's soul and worldview is complete. There is no doctrinal or theological way for him "back to God." Words and concepts have no currency in this dimension of pain, where the scarred heart is encapsulated in an impenetrable steel vault. This is not the place of resentment, bitterness, or even rage. Perhaps those are future partners.

There is no help from Job, because his is a Disneyland story of "happily ever after."

If the gospel makes any sense at all, if it has anything to offer this world, it is in the shattered existence of Larry. The incarnation, God with us, "Immanuel." And if the church has any ultimately meaningful role, it is to be the comforting arms of Jesus in the devastation of Larry's life. "God with Larry." This is the profound treasure and purest essence of the Christian truth. We have misunderstood the gospel if we diminish its function to a sorting-house for eternal destinations. The incarnation, the Immanuel event if you will, is the fulfillment of humanity's most poignant aspiration. This miracle event was not just a doctrinal occurrence, it is the substance of our faith and the most glorious ongoing fact of our daily existence. We are continually aching and grasping for the Spirit's invasion of our desperate lives.

We can hope and pray that Larry will somehow find Immanuel in the ruins of his life. And we can pray for ourselves, that somehow we would be able to reach down inside the prison of his existence and take on enough of his pain to hurt alongside him. Perhaps as we do so we can begin to create a space of tenderness and quiet where the devastated soul can escape the crushing questions that press in, a space where he can simply be held by Jesus.

Eventually Larry will face the arduous process of grieving the loss of his beautiful bride and best friend. He will have to walk through the dark valley with his son Tom, who will never erase the mental video clip of a mother destroyed and the memory of washing her unexplained misery from the walls of the kitchen where once blueberry muffins and afternoon banter gave definition and warmth to a family at peace and alive.

Oh, how we need Jesus.

I have watched the miracle of resurrection, of devastated lives made whole. I have stood there as people emerged from the tomb of their souls, and in them I have seen a mystical presence that is beyond the reach of my experience of Christ—a humble strength and gentleness that carries its pain, somehow, with dignity and an earthy heavenliness. Yes, it is Immanuel all over again, the incarnation revisited. It is Sunday morning after the cursed Friday, and the village is once again at dance.

There is no sane person who would voluntarily ask for the devastating experience of hell. But there is no saner person than the one who by fate has been to hell and emerged upon a higher ground.

8

Disapproval

Charlene believes she is trash.

Her misfortune was twofold: Dad did not want another child, and Dad did not want a disabled child. The second marriage was supposed to be a Hollywood sort of partnership in which man and woman live out a spontaneous succession of passionate plunges and foreign excursions, with the only limitation being the ability to get up for the next round of adult fun.

Of course, Charlene had no choice in her arrival—her father was directly responsible for the life in her mother's womb—and neither was she responsible for her inability to walk and talk with the same ease as her peers. This did not matter to Dad: Charlene was not wanted, and she would have to absorb the anger of Dad's ruined dreams.

Madison Avenue floods us with messages concerning the importance of winning the approval of our peers. All sorts of products are offered to help in this quest—from name-brand shoes to remade breasts—and to a large extent, we are all working each day under the invisible pressure of achieving the favor and acceptance of the significant others in our lives.

But Madison Avenue is nowhere near as effective as a disgruntled, selfish parent. The messages of Charlene's worthlessness are transmitted in every frequency possible. Besides the barrage and variety of verbal "you're-no-good" statements, Charlene carries with her three unforgettable experiences: She was tied to a post in the basement for an entire weekend while Dad went off on one of his flings; her own feces were forced down her throat after she had embarrassed Dad with an untimely bowel movement; and when she was five he attempted to drown her in the bathtub but was distracted by a persistent doorbell. Try to climb inside the consciousness of a five-year-old trapped underwater by Father's fierce grip about the neck.

Charlene is unable to see herself in any way except through the abuse and rejection of home. Her low self-esteem leads her to believe that God disapproves of her, and her very tender heart is fertile ground for the fiery messages from the pulpit that remind her every Sunday that God is displeased with our inability to meet divine standards. For her it is a fact: She was put together wrong; her very being is undesirable, and she must adjust to this status as if given a life sentence.

The typical cruel jabs that came from peers at school and Sunday school reinforced the truth of her undesirability. Hers is a lonely, empty cage of pain that grows larger than an abandoned warehouse with each day's encounter with the beautiful and loved people.

Recently, while spending a month in South Africa, I attended a small church service in Khayelitsha. This black settlement created by the government to hold laborers for the benefit of white industry is a million-person squalor whose conditions are not fit for the typical American's dog. The Khayelitsha graveyard is the most telling indicator of the quality of life in the black suburb—nearly every grave marker of this year's several thousand victims of poverty is for a child under four years old.

As I sat through the service, listening to the black pastor recount tales of God's goodness, I noticed a poster on the schoolroom bulletin board that cautioned citizens not to pick flowers. "It's against the Law," the poster warned, and a large daisy filled the frame with brilliant spring colors.

Ironic that the government that claims the authority of God to maintain the killing system of apartheid should make it against the law to pick daisies: Every day the system picks more of God's creation—people—and crushes them underfoot in the machinery of legalized oppression. Well, it is against God's law to pick people. They are beautiful creations of the Most High, and yet too many are subjected, like Charlene, to the abuse of people who have the power to bring misery.

God never gives authority to one human being to crush another. We are all created with equal dignity, and the law of love requires that all our deeds toward another celebrate this most basic fact of God's creation. Unfortunately, like Charlene, black Christians in South Africa have been reared with a double message concerning the acceptance of God. I have spoken with countless black Christians who from the cradle up have received the message that God created some with more dignity than others and that God in fact does have favorites. Every day's experiences of abuse at the hands of a white-church-run system underline that message. Should we be surprised that so many blacks find attraction in Islam, which promises them equality before God? Or that others prefer an atheistic form of government, in which Christianity would not be permitted to impose its denigrating message and system upon blacks?

In our religious socialization we are always quick to notice the errors of others' systems—for example, socialism or communism. But we are loath to accept that we are capable of inflicting identical wounds, if not worse, on the crown of God's creation—people. We claim the blanket approval of God for our systems and deeds and face the same danger as the people of Israel, who haughtily continued their abuse of the alien and stranger because they were sure God had ordained their system of government. What do we think Christ was suggesting when he told us to take the tree out of our own eye before trying to pry the itty-bitty speck out of another's?

Those who live as victims of the disapproval of others can find deep comfort in the story of Jesus. He is the perfect, unimprovable being. There is nothing we can add to his character to make him better or more appealing to the cries of the soul, no Madison Avenue insight that could help him achieve higher human dignity. Yet we are told in Scripture that he was *despised* and *rejected.* He was not, by the culture's standards, nice.

If Jesus was rejected by the dominant culture and the religious establishment, how much more we can expect it. Jesus' friends— note that I didn't say "projects"—were the despised and culturally marginalized. In your experience of being shut out by the beautiful people, you are accepted into the membership of Christ's community.

Anne told me her story of being forced to resign from the staff of one of this nation's largest evangelistic ministries. The reason was that she had become too overweight. Never mind that slander, striving for power, and the accumulation of wealth characterize daily dealings at the vice-presidential level of this ministry (I am well acquainted with the organization): Anne's looks did not fit in a structure that wanted to project a successful image to the public in order to raise funds for world evangelization. Apparently God had a wonderful plan for her life, but not when she was a few kilos too heavy. Her wrongful dismissal would easily win a hefty settlement in the secular court, where even "carnal" people would be clear-headed on the abuse she was dealt.

Take a quick survey of the line-up of Christian stars. Look at the platform, the Christian TV stations, the funds appeals by relief and development organizations, and the evangelistic ministries. All elevate the lifestyles of the pretty, rich, white, and famous. Too often our Christian structures have been seduced by the cultural versions of success and beauty, and as a consequence we have lost the fact of human dignity. People are not worthy beings because heaven resides within their frames; rather, they are worthy when they advance our corporate goals, stir us up with pride, affirm our values, and enhance our way of living.

Not so with the despised and rejected one who created us.

If you live with the disapproval of the church, find comfort in the fellowship of Jesus. The Scriptures tell us that he has loved us with an everlasting love, that he wants to draw us to him with an everlasting kindness. God created us in love, stood back to look at the final work of love, and pronounced it perfect.

We are simply unable to win the approval of God—we have it. God is the perfect parent who has given up everything in order to win us. The most illogical fact of our existence is that God literally wants to spend the entire eternity (a few billion years for starters) with us. God anticipates enjoying our companionship, and we can with confidence know that our loving parent enjoys us now.

Take comfort in Scripture—words the Spirit took care to breathe into the minds of the biblical writers:

> How great is the love the Father has lavished on us, that we should be called the children of God! And that is what we are!
>
> —1 John 3:1

> They will be my people, and I will be their God. I will give them singleness of heart and action, so that they will always fear me for their own good and the good of their children after them. I will make an everlasting covenant with them: I will never stop doing good to them, and I will inspire them to fear me, so that they will never turn away from me. I will rejoice in doing them good and will assuredly plant them in this land with all my heart and soul.
>
> —Jeremiah 32:38–41

You are Christ's prized possession, the showcase item that he pulls from the cabinet with care and delight as he brags on you, his child, to the angels. They marvel at his tender love for you— they don't understand this parental stuff of puffed-up chest and gleaming eye. They look forward to the eventual meeting in glory when they'll touch this wonderful creation of the God-parent.

In the meantime, as you slog down the road of recovery, learning to reject the lies of those who have picked you and crushed you underfoot, have hope in the fact that "the Lord is close to the brokenhearted and saves those who are crushed in spirit" (Psalm 34:18). No doubt it is a long and difficult road toward the healing that will restore to us the dignity robbed from us by family, friends, and the religious system. But one day we will be able to accept that Jesus approves of us and loves us with all his heart.

It is not an overused statement, and it is absolutely theologically sound: Jesus makes no junk.

Welcome to the company of people who have found Jesus' love. His family just keeps growing. Bask in the sunshine of his approval, let your soul thaw in the warmth of his delight over you. You are the special, unique, irreplaceable child of God, and the price Jesus paid to snatch you from the clutches of the impostor parent was, literally, hell.

And he would do it again.

9

Disappointment

Everyone has heard the story of the young girl who brings home a near-perfect report card and, beaming with pride, hands it to Dad: A+, A+, A+, A+, B-. "Why did you get a B-?" Dad asks. Or the son who performs his absolute best and brings home a report card of all C+'s and one D. Mom, sure that her son is just "unwilling to apply himself" in school, threatens to put a one-semester ban on Nintendo if he doesn't show the desire to buck up. Her best, his best. It's not good enough.

Competition, first prize, achievement, recognition. These represent the spirit and goal of our society. From the youngest age we are trained to measure our performance against others' expectations of us. We are schooled in the rat race of doing in order to be well spoken of, and a pursuit's value is measured not by its inherent worth but according to the public's scale of what is significant and what is not. Studies at school are not for the value of learning, for the sheer enjoyment of growing in understanding. Rather, they are to teach us how to get ahead, they are a measure of our worth, and, not insignificant, they are a mechanism to boost (or diminish) our parents' pride.

Childrearing, caring for an elderly neighbor, fixing engines at a mechanic shop—all of our living is done in the context of what others perceive to be the value of our labors. It is almost impossible in this context to hear the quiet voice of divine pleasure in a life privately and nobly lived for God, and the church has too often supported the status quo in this regard.

When was the last time your pastor grandstanded the blue-collar worker, the Central American alien laborer, or the grocery-bag stuffer as a wonderful Christian who is living wholesomely for Jesus? What TV preacher is bumping celebrities from the roster of guests in exchange for the "nobodies" who send in a large percentage of their social security check each month?

The majority of us are failures by both our culture's and our church's standards.

A friend of mine from Africa, Conrad, expressed his refreshing disbelief at an encounter he had at a church growth conference in Chicago. People were sharing their pilgrimages with each other in small groups. One of the participants told how he felt he had been a "bad testimony" because the business venture he founded several years earlier had collapsed. My friend's immediate and surprised response was, "How can you be so materialistic as to measure your testimony against the performance of a company?" It had never occurred to Conrad that God would look upon a person's heart through the fruits of a business enterprise.

Of course, we North Americans don't find that assumption at all surprising, because we have been raised—socialized, that is—to connect material advancement with God's blessing. Conrad's view is completely off the charts as far as our training is concerned—this was one of those educational cross-cultural encounters that shed light on the degree to which our culture's values have affected us. "Are many Americans that materialistic?" Conrad asked me.

Hmmm.

When last did your pastor or Robert Schuller or Pat Robertson or Fred Price put someone up front to tell the story of how he or she failed in business and now everything is gone—car, house, and company? No good ending of how the Lord came through, blessed me with much more than before, brought me through the fiery trial back to success. No, now I just work for the local school district as a janitor. In fact, how many janitors are on your church's governing board?

It is heartbreaking to meet Christians who have served with their best efforts but have not succeeded in fulfilling the expectations of those around them.

I have a friend, Dale, who worked for a lobbying organization in Washington, D.C., for seven years. He had been hired by the small nonprofit organization to create a credible Christian voice in the corridors of Congress on specific issues that were of biblical concern. Dale served on a shoestring budget that looked more like a missionary budget. Seven years later, he had very little to show for the effort except a sizable debt for the corporation. The board of directors unceremoniously and ungratefully dumped him, leaving him with the distinct message that he was no good and unwanted. Certainly one might ask, "Did his talents fit the skills required for the task?"—and the answer is no. But the board had hired him, and the board had approved his budget and activities over a seven-year period. They did not accept the ultimate responsibility for the organization's health.

Nor were they big enough people to graciously reward Dale's selfless efforts on their behalf—he had forsaken educational opportunities, financial security, and quality family time in pursuit of the board's goals. Rather than carefully and lovingly reviewing his progress and capabilities, they shunned him for his failures to perform, blamed him for the company's problems, and withdrew their affection.

Dale should have been been moved on to a position that complemented his skills and gifting. But it never should have been done in a manner that denied the dignity of his service to the ministry's goals all those years. He is left with the disappointment of having let the board down, and the board members are left with a smug sense of having rid themselves of the problem.

Most of us can easily name a dozen people who have given their best and have been asked by the condemning religious establishment why it wasn't all A+'s—whatever that would look like. By our standards, Jesus and all his disciples would be resounding failures.

Two thoughts are primary if you are one of those bashed-about servants who feels the intense disapproval of church and God for your labors. First, the *value* of your labor is measured quite simply by its having been performed out of love to the Lord. No one else can measure its significance. The ministry of financial support will illustrate: The men who poured bags of gold into the temple coffers quickly lined themselves up for positions of influence and respect. Jesus wasn't impressed. He noticed the widow who gave what to others was just a measly mite. It would never advance the building program of the temple or elevate her to a management committee. But as far as Jesus was concerned she had given more. How relevant do you suppose that story is for us today in our super-materialistic society? Perhaps Jesus had us in mind as much as anyone when he ensured it was recorded in Holy Writ.

Some are blessed with certain public skills or gifts of management, and others—perhaps you are one of them—suffer by the comparison. Take comfort in the lesson of the widow's mite.

Second, we need to hear that life is packed with stumbling. What parent (what sensible and loving one, that is) scolds an eighteen-month-old child for tripping while trying to deliver some goodies to Mom? The sincere and childlike delight of giving is what stirs the parent heart, and so it is with our heavenly parent. Anyone who has tried to live for God has failed. In fact, I would venture to say that if you cannot list several instances of stumbling, you have not yet lived by faith for Jesus.

We need to know that whereas our culture and church have often left us in that lonely place of failure, of having disappointed them and failed to meet their standards of performance, God looks on us with *pleasure*. God loves our deeds-from-the-heart and, yes, is showing off pictures of you to the angels on a galaxy-wide TV screen. You never made it on *700 Club*—so what?

I don't want to sound flippant, as that may belittle the pain. But we have to remember that the materialistic, pride-based standards of our society don't matter. They are nothing; one day they will be ravaged by the flames. Jesus is so upside-down that he claims it is possible to burn at the stake for the sake of the gospel or to give our lives on behalf of the poor but to have done nothing for him—because it was not done in love. The widow's mite was given in love, and so was your labor that now goes unrewarded.

Often we are left with a profound confusion or disorientation when handed the disappointment of others whom we served. And we experience the confusion of God's role in our pain: Didn't we pray for specific guidance? Didn't we move into our ministry position out of a clear sense of the Holy Spirit's nudging? Didn't we relinquish all other attractive options because of God's priorities and biblical commands? Our very theological base, once again, is shattered, and we are left with the task not only of recovering the dignity of our past service but also of reorienting our perception of God's involvement and interest in the specifics of our lives.

Your relief will come.

Take heart in these Scriptures:

> They reeled and staggered like drunken men;
> they were at their wits' end.
> Then they cried out to the Lord in their trouble,
> and he brought them out of their distress.
> He stilled the storm to a whisper;
> the waves of the sea were hushed.
> They were glad when it grew calm,
> and he guided them to their desired haven.
> —Psalm 107:27–30

Perhaps you are also struggling with the feeling that you have failed Jesus. If so, you need to hear that even if you somehow lost faith in the trial of attempting to live for him, Jesus will not and cannot forsake his own child:

> If we died with him,
>> we will also live with him;
> if we endure,
>> we will also reign with him.
> If we disown him,
>> he will also disown us;
> if we are faithless,
>> he will remain faithful,
>> for he cannot disown himself.
>> —2 Timothy 2:11–13

Hold fast to the dignity of your giving. Have courage to go through the difficult territory of rediscovering your gifts and calling, of sorting out God's voice in your call to labor from all the competing voices that clamor for your service. This is all a natural part of our discipleship process and does not diminish your love labor to this point.

Listen to Yahweh:

> The Lord your God is with you,
>> he is mighty to save.
> He will take great delight in you,
>> he will quiet you with his love,
>> he will rejoice over you with singing.
>> —Zephaniah 3:17

So pick up the spilled cookies and keep stumbling your way across the living room floor to Mom. She cannot conceal the pleasure she experiences in your deed.

10

Distance

"Seek me and I will be found. Call upon me and I shall answer," says the Lord.

What about the silence? What about all the crying out for help when all that follows is the ricochet of your own voice off the walls of your prison of pain?

Dealing with wounds inflicted by people is bad enough; add to that the inability to connect with God, and we are nearly devastated. Evangelicals have not been very good at understanding the silence of God, and consequently we have too often been guilty of heaping additional burdens on the already burdened brother or sister. "God will not hear you if you regard sin in your heart," you may be counseled. So for the hundredth time you rehearse all the sin of your youth to God, in case you left something out before. Confession is reduced to a legalistic game of finally piling up just the right amount of sin so that the door to Christ will open up once again. And instead of sensing the love of God in our time of pain,

we sink lower into depression, for now we also bear the false condemnation that God is distant from us because we are not
adequately facing our fallenness.

Yet nothing could be farther from the truth.

As difficult as it is to understand given our traditions, at times
God's love for us is best expressed in absolute silence. Our experience of it at first is the active withrawal of God's voice, an
ever-widening chasm that seems to put us further and further out
of God's reach. God has backed away and apparently does not
love us any more. Somehow we have offended our Maker, and
God will from now on be merely a distant doctrinal concept; we
will have a legal relationship based on the blood of Calvary, but
the joy that used to accompany the courtship has forever fled.

The fear, even panic, associated with this phenomenon is not
unlike that felt in a marriage where one spouse just decides to quit
talking, giving no reason. "Have I offended him in some grave
manner?" "Is she having an affair?" "Is he planning to leave me
and just isn't saying why?" The silence creates a barrier to understanding. The longer the silence, the worse the projected fears.

We open our Bible for our regular quiet time, and nothing speaks
to us. At church on Sunday, during worship, we sing all the familiar choruses and watch the others around us beam with the warmth
of God's love—and for us there is simply nothing. The pastor de-
livers a passionate sermon that obviously stirs the congregation
beyond its usual level of repentance and healing, and we stand
there afterward thinking we might as well have been at an Amway
sales meeting—it was just a bunch of hype.

If this is your experience, you may very well have entered what
some call the "dark night of the soul." Dating back to St. John of
the Cross, this phrase refers to the maddening silence of God during our time of greatest need. The term is familiar within the Roman
Catholic tradition but not enough so to Protestants, and therefore
we are more likely to sense the judgment of Christians around us
during this time of distance.

This prison, the silence of God, our dark night, becomes ours
most typically as a consequence of ministry circumstances that
exhaust or deeply hurt us, or after we experience a profound loss,

say the death of a child. Perhaps you have struggled with the feelings of somehow having failed God in ministry, or you are still reeling from the pain of being stabbed in the back by other Christians after years of faithful service. And then it is God's silence. Driven into despair through the pain, you are now best described as being on a downward spiral that leads deeper into hell.

It is curious how we maintain our materialism even after becoming Christians. It is obvious that if we have asked Christ to become our Lord and Savior, we believe there is a spirit world that cannot be accessed throught material means. And yet when we no longer sense God in the familiar material, emotional encounters, we say God is not there.

There are paths to God that cannot be followed through the familiar. When we are lost in the distance of God, we are left to the frantic struggle of searching out ways to know God that to this point we have not discovered. There is a withdrawal, a moving away from all that has put us in touch with God before, and then an awful silence.

God is speaking to us forcefully during these times, but we have yet to learn that voice. God is coming to us through another medium that is beyond our experience. Whereas we have been trained to actively employ the disciplines of spirituality that call God up to rescue us, now we wait for that totally effortless, passive encounter with God that cannot happen to us through the active pursuit of the divine voice.

I believe this is a profound privilege for us. Our encounters with pain have been intense and destructive, and God now comes to us in a manner that matches the depth of our pain. Our senses are stilled as we wait, and our desperation increases as the silence persists.

Nothing.

The silence becomes oppressive as it crushes in on our empty soul. We have endured months of no voice, and it is as though our soul is a drained water pouch that will collapse if nothing fills the void soon. We are a body without food, even though we go through the exercise, three times each day, of eating.

There is absolutely nothing.

Faith, we are told, is the evidence of things not seen. The distance we feel from God after the encounter of pain is an opportunity for faith. Listen to Jeremiah:

> Yet this I call to mind
>   and therefore I have hope:
> Because of the Lord's great love we are not consumed,
>   for his compassions never fail.
> They are new every morning;
>   great is your faithfulness.
> I say to myself, "The Lord is my portion;
>   therefore I will wait for him."
>
> The Lord is good to those whose hope is in him,
>   to the one who seeks him;
> it is good to wait quietly
>   for the salvation of the Lord.
>   —Lamentations 3:21–26

Sit in your void. Wait out the suffocating silence. And listen.

In time you will find the presence of God in language you do not understand. You will fellowship with God in a dimension of the real that up to this point was not available even to your imagination. Your soul will meet the eternal as you are pulled away into the heavenlies and then thrust back to the earth. Glory has reached down to your level of pain and embraced you with a knowledge of the holy that more than matches the darkness of your distance. You are a new person, as was John, who spoke of being taken away to the seventh heaven, where he saw unspeakable wonders that filled his prison cell on Patmos to his death. No amount of distance was now great enough to remove him from the presence of the throne. No amount of dark could now snuff out the marvelous light.

You will watch the emissaries of condemnation scatter under the persistence of *your* new light, and as the Spirit lifts you to a new plane of experiencing God, you will be transformed from glory unto glory, and the darkness will bemoan its prisoner set free.

Indeed you will, by waiting, have silenced the silence.

11

Spiritual Codependency

Let me risk a harsh image: There are victims of pain who keep going back to their victimizers. It is the picture of a teenage daughter who is regularly sexually abused by the father; yet she is emotionally dependent on her dad's affirmation, so she keeps going into his bedchamber. Too many Christians have this sort of relationship with the church.

It may be a shock to think of the church in those terms, yet if you have been severely hurt by the church, for your own health and recovery you need to demythologize it. In its most human form, the church is nothing more than a corporation whose leaders have figured out how to avoid government control and taxes. Incorporation documents are filed with the government, as with a secular company; a president, treasurer, and secretary are elected, as with a secular company; money is charged in exchange for services (churches call it offerings—businesses call it fees), and staff are hired, fired, promoted, and trained; buildings are erected, brochures are printed, and salaries are increased as profits grow.

The church, however, claims three distinctive roles—one, it is there to help men and women draw closer to God; two, it is to be in the world as the community of God, serving as salt and light in society; and three, its very structure was created and ordained by God to have spiritual authority over the "sheep."

All of us know people who have been hurt by a pastor. All of us know pastors who are bad for their congregations. Yet our fear of the ethereal, holy, spiritual dimension of church bars us from being able to see the pastor (and the members of the board) as fully human, fully fallible, and just as flawed in his or her pursuit of God as we, the parishioners, are.

Dysfunctional relationships require at least two partners—those who exert their power and abuse on another and those who have a perceived need that is being met by the abuser. You find this in spouse-to-alcoholic-spouse relationships, father-to-abused-daughter, and general-to-nonthinking-private. On the spiritual plane you find it in the relationship between God's leader and the God-needy layperson.

It is the sincere young Christian who is most vulnerable to this abuse. The fresh, uninitiated heart wants nothing more than to please God—to do what is right. And here is a person of God, much older in the faith, commanding a large following, who claims to have authority from God to lead the "flock." Cult leaders, of course, are the simplest illustration of this point: Jim Jones was able to lead several hundred into suicide because he spoke for God.

Put your mind and fears aside and go like sheep to the slaughter.

We are capable of wielding similar influence over others in the name of faithfulness to Christ.

Ever think about how strange it is for a pastor or organizational leader to preach on his or her authority from God and our corresponding need to willingly follow? What else but a haughty, puffed-up sense of self could call for the spiritual subservience of adults? It is nothing more than shameful manipulation that demands others' allegiance because of some sense of spiritual authority: "Stop thinking about the issues, don't worry, trust me. I've been into the inner chambers with God, and I know that as strange as this all sounds, it's good for you."

How refreshing it would be to hear a pastor say: "I would like to build a new sanctuary. Now if you people had any self-respect at all, you would tell me I am crazy to propose that you all cut back the comfort of your lives in order to build us a big building. If you had sense you'd tell me I need to drop the idea or go find a new job. Listen, I do not speak for God any more than you do, so I cannot claim his vote on this issue. But I'd like you to humor me and give me a chance to make my case. I'd like to convince you that it is worth all the extra money it is going to take because it will, in my opinion, help in the pursuit of the goals God has put on all our hearts."

Instead, too often we hear that God spoke to the pastor in a time of prayer and that those who want to get with the Lord's program now have this unique chance to get with the Spirit. Show your desire for the Lord's way: Get out of the pew and demonstrate your faith with your checkbook. How strange it would be if at the annual stockholders' meeting the president explained the need for the stockholders just to trust his judgment on the planned expansion, because he has a supernatural skill that the others do not in projecting what is good for the company.

The greater percentage of my time in the past ten years has been spent in the mission industry. This is the world I grew up in, and I love it with my heart. I hope for many more good years linked to the enterprise. The most sincere and committed Christians you will find anywhere in the world pass through there—they are ready to give their very lives to the cause of bringing Christ's love to those who have not heard. What could be purer? Yet there is a dreadfully dark side to this industry that feeds on souls of dysfunctional people who are ready to do whatever Christ calls them to. I have seen mission leaders twist the Scriptures, publish false figures, distort history, and slander other groups—all in the name of and for the sake of influencing you to give your money, your time, and your very body to their cause. Nothing else is as important to God's heart, they tell you: If you want God's affection, get with the program.

Agency XYZ claims that it is The Center for God's global purposes and if you'd just plug into its scheme of things Christ would come back soon. I have interviewed too many first-term missionaries who on furlough came to realize that they were nothing more than pawns in the idealistic scheme of some megalomaniac who claimed to speak for God. One organization claims it can reach the entire world for Jesus with its scheme of dividing the globe into five thousand population groups. Another has it divided into twelve thousand. The only thing keeping Jesus from coming back is our unwillingness to join the program. If we'd apply simple faith it could happen. All dissenting voices are labeled as lacking vision and hope.

Humility is not a virtue in these circles. Neither is honesty.

You may be one of those who have spent the last ten years of their lives living out someone else's dream. You were convinced that nothing was closer to God's heart, and now you understand it for what it was. You grieve the loss of all the wasted years and hate the fact that you so easily and readily submitted to the organization's grand designs on your life.

Our human need for love and affection almost defies description. We will pursue love with more energy than any other prize. This is particularly true of those who have been starved of affection in their youth: We regularly require reassurance of our worth, and are constantly downgrading ourselves to others. We do not have the ability to care for ourselves (we have difficulty perceiving what our needs are), and we always feel helpless. The sad fact regarding people who were reared under such cruel conditions is that they seem to lack the ability to stay away from that which hurts them. Again, it's the daughter returning to the abusing father.

I have chosen the term "spiritual codependency" to characterize some of our pain, because I believe that when you put together the ego-driven Christian leader with the love-starved Christian layperson who longs for the affection of Father, you have the occasion of one obsessively returning to the source of abuse. The church heaps burdens on you, calls you to fulfill its agendas, asks for extreme sacrifice to complete the programs of God (and secure the Lord's pleasure), and so you keep going back for more.

You become worn-out and hurt, and because you are not aware of your codependent link to church, you increase your commitments in order to (spiritually) care for yourself. Instead of getting better, you do precisely the thing that hurt you in the first place, so you become all the more damaged. The grace of God is probably more critical in this cage of pain than in any other context.

It has already been said in this book, but in your case it is especially important, that you must pray for the grace to see yourself as God sees you—a splendid, totally accepted, prized creation who is unable to do any more to win the affections of Father or Mother. And pray for grace to care for yourself—to silence the haunting voice of the past and the forceful voice of the present that would tell you to work, slave, achieve, wear yourself out, and then finally rest only once you have burned out.

This is no short journey. It is as though your soul were a sponge the size of a city. It badly needs to soak up the love of Jesus and is almost insatiable in this regard. Even though you will regularly hear God's love story for you, there will be entire regions of your life that must hear that truth in new ways. Each cell of your sponge soul must experientially know it for a fact—it cannot be transferred intellectually from other compartments of your soul.

Be patient with the process, and don't fall back on the security of your old serving ways.

Beware of commitment language. Yes, God has called us to give our lives for kingdom purposes, Jesus has bought us at a price, we are no longer our own. But God has not given any other human being on this earth the power to define what that commitment looks like in your specific case. You will need the grace to sit back—entirely uninvolved in the outward activities of radical committed living—to pass into the secure silence of God and there to rest in love. In the quiet of the Spirit's presence you will learn anew to hear God's commands, to feel God's nudgings. When you finally go forward to serve, it will not be out of the need to win divine affection. Rather, it will come from the deep assurance that you already have that affection. Your labors will be the wholesome response of one who wants to give to others the gift of grace and love that has been so wonderfully experienced in your own life. This labor will not be a drudgery, it will be a delight. You will not serve as one in bondage, but rather as one who is marvelously free.

Let Jesus rejoice over you. Sit back and take it in. Enjoy the vacation-of-grace, and deny any human being (including yourself) the vile pleasure of winning your labors in exchange for God's love.

12

Bitterness

Bitterness is the deadly virus of the soul.

It enters our system through the betrayal of others and then is left to accomplish its destructive work long after the violator has moved out of our immediate life. It is in this regard the cruelest of all pain, because it is effective to remind us each moment of our waking hours that we are the worthless playground of others' exploits, and it lingers to destroy us bit by bit—rather than with the swift and decisive swoosh of the guillotine.

First the emotions are ravaged, then the energy is drained, next the hatred mounts, and the soul is poisoned by its need for revenge. Finally the spirit is suffocated: Bitterness has achieved its master's work.

Don't let it.

All the complex emotions related to pain must run their course if we are to experience true healing, but bitterness is not one of them. It is enemy occupation of your heart, and you must deny it any territorial gain.

Resentment and bitterness are cousins, but it is bitterness that works for the destruction of our souls. Resentment recognizes an injustice for what it is. It is, in a sense, a true measure of the degree of pain inflicted on us.

A woman is denied a leadership position in a Christian organization simply because her physiological equipment is not the same as the man's at the helm: She has the talents, the educational credentials, the work experience, and the positive reviews by former employers. She is a victim of sexism.

Resentment locates the specific injustice and calls it what it is. It is the honest and genuine inventory of the wrong committed. Christians who would counsel you to rush past the sensitivities that resentment bring to the crime don't actually believe in the gravity of the criminal act. To resent the action of another is to tell the truth of something that has been illegitimately denied you or taken from you.

We are to resent the deeds of darkness because they bring pain where God intended health; darkness where God intended light; destruction where God intended life. Resentment is the indignation we feel toward a system that easily kills its citizens, as in the communist purge of students at Tiananmen Square in 1989, or the racist purge of contradictory voices in South Africa. In our country we experience this indignation over the wanton destruction of millions of babies in the womb or the suppression of the human rights of ethnic minorities. We resent the actions that trample the dignity of others—resentment is as central to our gifting in the Holy Spirit as any part of gifting.

In dealing with your bitterness, don't deny the reading on the barometer that resentment provides.

Bitterness has two chief expressions. One form focuses on the individuals or institutions that caused the pain. The notion of revenge is coddled and nurtured. No happy thoughts or warm wishes can be extended toward them. They deserve the worst; only then will peace come. This notion of peace with revenge is an entirely secular concept that is taught to us from the youngest years. When Rambo's friends have been unjustly taken by the enemy, securing their freedom is not enough—he needs to destroy a village or platoon in the course of action. Now injustice is avenged, and he can sleep in peace.

The truth is, by such an action one has only committed oneself further to the myth of revenge, and the next encounter with injustice will require an even greater act of retribution to satisfy the bitter heart. And it gets worse with each act of revenge. "Justice" gained by the destruction of the person or institution that inflicted the pain is not justice. It is the postulation that taking an eye for an eye reaffirms the dignity of your former, unviolated self, whereas it is actually reducing you to the same undignified place as the predator.

Bitterness can extend its reach beyond the individual or institution to the general population or to "life," and this is its second way of ex-pression. Life dealt you a bad hand, you insist. That may actually be true—for example, a child who is born with severe physical limitations has fewer opportunities to achieve the comforts of the American dream. Or a child who is born in the height of Ethiopia's famine is deprived of essential nutrients for the development of body and mind. The consequences are experienced for the rest of this person's life.

In this case, bitterness can fail to see any good in life and will seek a false sense of peace and fulfillment through the destruction of institutions that had nothing to do with the injustice the victim bears.

To put aside the power of bitterness is in no way to deny the gravity of evil committed against yourself; rather, it is to deny evil the power to commit additional crimes against you.

The decision to let go of bitterness will be fraught with ambivalence, because we will be struggling with the conditioning that has taught us that healing is experienced through revenge. We will feel the loss of a remedy for our pain—not because it *is* a remedy, but because we thought it was a remedy. In some ways, saying no to bitterness has more to do with faith than it does with holiness. We are trusting God that it will be good for us. We have also been trained, consciously or unconsciously, that to forgo revenge is to be silent on the crime, and worse, to give it legitimacy (to cancel the crime, retribution must match the gravity of the violation). It may be more right-side-up, however, to ask whether our vengefulness makes us look more like the predator and therefore diminishes the degree of evil committed against us.

We need to let Jesus meet us at our point of weakness as we face bitterness. Its powerful, demonic pull is not easy to overcome. Jesus promises us relief:

> His divine power has given us everything we need for life and godliness through our knowledge of him who called us by his own glory and goodness.
>
> —2 Peter 1:3

> He gives strength to the weary and increases the power of the weak.
>
> —Isaiah 40:29

There is only one effective medicine against the poison of bitterness, and it is forgiveness. The longer we have nurtured our bitterness, the more difficult the road to forgiveness. But then, too, forgiveness cannot be rushed or contrived. Often the ministry of forgiveness has been preached to us as a requirement for holiness. That is only partially true. Yes, we must learn forgiveness, because it is the means to understand the forgiveness we have received. It is also the path toward freedom, allowing us to ask Jesus to continue forgiving us. But rather than demanding forgiveness of a broken person as another one of the "requirements" of righteousness, it is much more accurate and compassionate to describe forgiveness as both a road map away from danger and a gift that comes from the outside.

Let me explain. If my child is not aware of the danger of freight trains and is too young to judge the safe distance from train tracks, I will, simply out of love for my child, forbid him to play near the tracks. I have put in front of him a requirement—I demand compliance for his sake. Christ calls us to forgiveness because he knows we are in danger of death without it. So we must not be burdened by its demand as a measure of our holiness; consider it instead a sign that points us away from the railroad track. In time, as the hurt heals, we will experience grace to understand forgiveness as our friend and as a reflection of the character of Christ resident in us.

And forgiveness is a gift. How cruel to heap guilt for unforgiveness upon someone who has experienced the savage act of rape. The victim is victimized even more. No, forgiveness is a gift of the Holy Spirit, and we will find that we must wait for it. It seems to me that forgiveness will be genuine as it contemplates the gravity of the evil committed, and as such it is a multilayered process. We will continually be forgiving the criminal, because we will continue to uncover the degree to which the crime has damaged us.

As a child, Derek was sexually abused by his mother. When he was a single man in college, he achieved forgiveness of her through some loving counsel from friends. It was not until several years later, however, that Derek was able to realize the extent of the damage. Recently married, he has discovered that he is unable to have a healthy sexual relationship with his delightful bride. They truly love each other but have been robbed of God's gift to them because of a crime committed by a mother. For Derek the work of forgiveness begins all over again, and with much more intensity than before.

Derek cannot just say, "OK, I forgive." The new level of pain is so intense that he simply hurts. And he wants to get rid of that pain through bitter revenge.

Jesus comes to Derek, not with requirements, but with the gift of forgiveness. Derek's heart can cry out for that gift in the middle of the pain, because Jesus says that he knows our pain—he has given us the right to run boldly into his presence and shout our pain while acknowledging that we cannot forgive. In fact, we are not sure we want to be able to forgive.

Here we must rest in the character and knowledge of Jesus. He will not destroy us because we have been wounded, and he knows our hearts better than we do. As we experience the condemnation of a heart sickened through pain, God looks at a heart begging for release. So take comfort in the hope that God will give you the gift of forgiveness. Wait in convalescence, be patient with the process, and one day wake up to the surprising realization that you have forgiven. You will run free. The fever will be gone. The strength will have returned. And yet another demonic design will have failed.

Is there any purer expression of the Spirit-filled life than the one who has been ravaged by the evil of another and yet chooses forgiveness over bitterness? I think not.

Welcome the honesty of resentment. Take refuge in the fact that there is no condemnation upon you from Christ as you live your pain. Pray for the gift of forgiveness that will free you from your predator and cleanse your soul.

13

Cynicism

Cynicism is given birth in the death of hope. It is the ultimate statement that no good can come of people or institutions, and it finally will lead to the death of faith.

Like bitterness, cynicism is not a transitory feeling that helps us identify our pain and takes us through the process of healing. Cynicism robs us of the miracles of life, the encounters with the supernatural hand of God in areas where the harsh blows of evil have left us mortally wounded. Cynicism is a statement that even the resurrection of Jesus Christ from the grave carries no meaning or power beyond its historical job of rescuing us from hell (if, the cynic wonders, there is such a thing as heaven).

This posture toward life is not arrived at through a mischievous intention to deny the possibility of God's intervening in history today. It is the logical outcome of horrendous pain inflicted on one—over and over again—of harm delivered where good was hoped for. The point of view of a cynic is as legitimate as any view of life, and therefore, if we are to be saved from its treacherous, destructive impact on our lives, we need to understand its origins.

If the cousin of bitterness is resentment, the cousin of cynicism is skepticism. Skepticism makes us wary of the promises people and structures offer us. It understands the pervasive nature of evil, knowing that even the most benign structures, such as the local church and mission agency, are capable of extremely destructive acts, be they intentional or not.

Skepticism is a warning system: It flashes the red lights and sounds the siren when we become too romantic in our attraction to structures, visions, or dreams. Skepticism asks questions, does not accept simple solutions, mistrusts those who claim to have the best ideas or the best understanding of the issues. Skepticism looks for ulterior motives in the purest of presentations and refuses to quit the argument merely to bring peace to the conversation.

Skeptics ruin our great speeches and plans, and we wish they would just go away. Why can't they shine in their little corner and I in mine? The reason is that despite harsh experiences of life, the skeptic has not given up hope on the possibility for light to overcome the darkness, for good men and women to prevail where angels fear to tread. These people are applying their faith toward a better future, and because they are investing themselves in it they want to enter with both eyes wide open, utilizing all the wisdom they have accumulated in life's school.

Perhaps the marked difference between a skeptic and a cynic is that the cynic has not had enough healthy encounters with the structures and leaders of this world to believe it is possible that people can and want to do good. Every time she has applied her faith she has been torched. Every ministry relationship turned out to be someone using him for a personal end, and every financial risk taken at the bidding of a sincere Christian resulted in loss.

Basically, the cynic concludes, people are going to rob you, use you, abuse you, and discard you. The wise person is the one who looks out for number one and allows very little or no emotional involvement in the possibilities of making this world a better place.

If our experiences at the hands of others have been particularly harsh, we have the option to choose between skepticism and cynicism. The latter harms us. We need to be assured that we have not lost anything healthy by opting for skepticism. We have, in fact, become healthier, because we have decided to use the lessons of our negative experiences rather than stay uninformed, choosing the ignorant route of cynicism.

Of all the emotions we are going to experience through the hardships of life, this is the one that requires the most faith from us. We cannot sit back and watch faith perform for us—we must exercise our faith. We have to be willing to go back down old roads of vision and expectation. We are actually returning to the place of pain and saying, "It didn't have to be so." It is easier to deny any value in our past pursuits or relationships and simply shut the door on those years as easily as we cap a garbage can. In the short term this quick-fix to pain will bring relief, but in the long run we will have robbed ourselves of certain tender encounters and genuine ministry opportunities that did in fact happen.

And again, time has a wonderful way of letting us heal as we go back to the areas of vulnerability. In Woody Allen's *Crimes and Misdemeanors* he reflects on the past by saying, "Tragedy plus time equals comedy." There are certain experiences of life for which this will be true. We will laugh at our gullibility, for the way we were so easily led down the rosy path. Such replays will become times of healing.

But there are hurts that never will fit into Woody Allen's formula for life's bummers. There are our most vulnerable parts that have been violated too many times and too deeply to become fodder for future levity. We must not insist any differently. We can let go of our cynicism while also asserting the truth of our pain.

As we enter the healing process, we will need to go to Jesus and rediscover him. We have been hurt by those who claim to be his ambassadors, and now we need to find out anew who Jesus really is. We will in time find him wholly trustworthy, and we will discover that he always acts toward us in love. Those who hurt us may have been acting toward us in full sincerity and good faith, but that does not negate the harmful substance of their deeds. Nothing but good flows from God, so we can confidently separate Jesus from the evil we have experienced.

We will watch him rebuild our broken lives and create a brand-new person who can celebrate the life-giving work of the Holy Spirit. In short, our best defense against cynicism in the future will be the fact that *we* are now the product of his miraculous hand—and what he did in us he can do in others too.

We are probably more right than wrong when we conclude that organizations are not capable of good. They have a way of propagating their own life as the highest good—and pity the persons in the way of their forward movement. The organized church is not exempt from this tendency. Indeed, there actually is no such thing as a "Christian structure." It is the life we put into these structures every day that determines whether it will be good for people or not. And a good behavior record today does not ensure good behavior tomorrow. Structures require aggressive, determined nurturing if they are to serve people well.

In our cynicism we can and must honestly recognize that there are many organizations (including the local church) that are filled with people who do want to behave as Christians in their approach to management and caring for the world. Rather than burdening others with the expectation that they live up to our standards of what makes an organization "Christian," rejoice whenever you see it happen. That incident is the miraculous kingdom of God at work, right in our midst, despite the efforts of the roaring lion that prowls about seeking and destroying.

If you don't let go of the weapon of cynicism, it will eventually turn on you. You will become your own best example of why nothing and nobody is trustworthy, and you will have to live out that viewpoint in order to put to death the insistent nagging of hope. Hope is all around us, quietly feeding the elderly, visiting the prisoners, caring for the unborn, working for the release of the oppressed. But hope is not a grandstand item on TV or in the pulpit, because it, too, is a skeptic. It mistrusts the motives of those who would boost it to national prominence. It labors *for* others, not in front of them, and its work is rarely noticed by those who value flashy success over humble service.

So you have to look for hope. It will be in the most surprising of places, and when you find it you will slide ever so little toward its appealing labors of love—till one day you look back at yourself and notice with delight that somewhere in the process of becoming whole you were quietly transformed into a tenderhearted skeptic. And the world will be a better place because of you.

Keep the faith.

14

Disillusionment

Disillusionment can eventually lead to cynicism, but the two are quite distinct in how they affect us.

Disillusionment is a loss. It is that dreadful time of sorrow when you grieve the death of dreams and visions of what could have been. And it is that lonely period of mourning the death of relationships with those who once were among your closest friends and coworkers in pursuing the big, exciting dreams that captured your heart.

Except for the physical death of a loved one, I don't know if there is a pain that is sharper or more penetrating than this wound to the heart. Fortunately for us, it is a process that will end, and there is a wonderful place of tenderness on the other side if we have the courage and will to face the anguish along the way.

Perhaps you know this pain.

You met Jesus at a "revival" meeting. There you were promised peace, joy, and happiness if you would only "give your heart" to the Savior. All of your problems (in fact, all of life's ills) derive from the evil heart, so turn it over to Jesus and watch the problems go away. You made the choice, you said no to old ways and friends, and you joined the group that led you to Christ. Your spirit of thankfulness for having the true way taught to you prompted you to serve the church leaders wherever they asked—from cleaning restrooms to watching the children at church functions—and you gave generously of your few and hard-earned dollars to the programs the minister said were critical to get the good news out to others. You became a devoted follower of the pastor, and, without knowing it, you became dependent: His or her compliments, anecdotes for problems, advice for daily living, and Sunday-morning sermons were your staple in your walk with Christ. When the pastor started a TV program from the church, you watched it every day with unswerving faithfulness, and you recruited many others to view the daily broadcast of inspiration and insight. And you continued to give.

One Sunday, more elders than usual are up front, and they all wear a grave look that has your curiosity stirred up. Perhaps there is some exciting plan they intend to share that will require more faith than you have ever exercised. After the second hymn and the offering, the pastor steps to the podium, and the elders form a semi-circle behind. "I have sinned"—the words push their way out through tight lips. "I have been unfaithful to my spouse and to the Lord. I will be moving out of my home this week. I am so sorry to have hurt you this way. As of today I am taking a leave of absence from the church to seek the Lord."

The pastor's slouched body shuffles to the exit, and the elders take over. They are saying words, but of course you don't hear them. Your sanctuary of tranquillity and holiness has just been smashed to bits, and you immediately face a tangled mess of emotions, from panic to betrayal to despair. The foundations upon which you built your religious experience are crumbling, and that sweet and sincere purity of the faith that has been your companion these several years is now powerless to reach you.

One day perhaps skepticism will help you laugh through the memories of your sincere youth (let's hope that cynicism will find no home in you), but for now you are sick from disillusionment.

Or perhaps your story is a little different. You never did have too rosy a view of the pastor or the church, but you did nonetheless heartily participate in all major church functions and gave generously because you understood human behavior well enough to know that we all stumble our way through this world together. You do believe that God will guide us in the "way we ought to go," and you are genuinely appreciative of the community and supportive role the church gives you in your walk with Jesus.

Only something starts to go wrong. Your husband starts to beat you. You haven't been cheating on him or in any way disregarding him, but he is in a time of struggle, and somehow he feels the permission to take out his frustrations on your body. This was never supposed to come with the package called Christian marriage. In fact, both of you took Contemporary Christian Marriage together at the Christian college where you met, and you carefully followed the advice of the professor: Regard the other as higher than yourself, serve one another, forgive, worship together, and always go to the Lord together in any major decisions.

Jim, your husband, is unable to quit. You fear the church's opinion of you and Jim's wrath if you go public on your problem, and your silence serves to sanction his actions. You were taught that women are supposed to submit to their husbands, and even though the Scriptures do not condone his behavior, you cannot commit what you were taught is the greater wrong of defying his authority and the indissoluble bond of marriage.

Several attempts at getting help from your pastor do not improve the marriage, and after five sessions with a therapist, all of which Jim scorns, the beatings continue.

You make the painful decision to leave Jim. Your understanding of Scripture does not approve of either Jim's beatings or your departure, but you have to care for yourself. Jim retaliates with the most obscene insults, and your pastor chastises you for not going the way of the Lord. He tells you that he will ask God to bring you back together, and he pleads with you to not pursue the divorce in order to maintain clear fellowship with God.

The Christian marriage didn't work. That was painful enough. And now the church banishes you from the inner circle of leaders,

Sunday school teachers, and mission committee. You are no longer fit to serve. You are given notice to discontinue all your official ministry roles because now you are not in a good position to influence others. You followed the biblical formula for successful Christian living, and now your life is a disillusioned mess.

Or your story may be that of an activist-on-the-rocks. Your commitment to Christ was exemplary from the youngest years, and no one was surprised when you announced your decision to be a missionary. The church deacons and women's prayer band were "pleased as punch," because there was no higher expression of your discipleship than to accept the challenge to cross-cultural ministry.

Raising support for the work in Asia was not difficult, and very soon you were on a plane to preach Christ where he was not known. A couple of years later you had successfully planted a church, and now you were doing the happy work of discipleship. But a strange discord began to develop between you and a senior mission leader. You did not understand the source of the tension, but you were clearly stepping on somebody's toes. Eventually you were confronted for insubordination, and the field council transferred you to another district. Your church was firm with you about the need to learn from the agency "elders," and they were pleased to see your teachable spirit. Support, both financial and verbal, continued to flow.

On your new assignment you discovered that nationals in your region were suffering terrible atrocities at the hand of the government. You began to listen to their stories, and soon your Bible came freshly alive as you found a whole new depth of God's compassion for the downtrodden. You publicly spoke your mind about the need for justice, and before long you were summoned once again to the missionary field council. They cautioned you against political involvement. You innocently shared with them your discovery of oppression and how it stirred you deeply to respond out of your love for Christ. You told them of your new biblical insights and the joy of representing those crushed by the harsh and unjust government system.

Once again they cautioned you to stay away from politics. You asked whether just standing by, watching the oppression and doing nothing, was not also a form of political involvement, a vote in favor of the government's deeds. You were barraged with a series of one-liners on the government's need to protect the nation from the "outside threat of communism"; they said if you really wanted to be serious about oppression, talk about the Soviet Union and Angola.

The real problem, you were beginning to sense, was not that you cared about the people's oppression, but that you had differing opinions on politics. Your attempts at communication with the field council produced no fruit, and a couple of months later you were cut off by your home church for having taken "this most disturbing turn toward politics, forsaking the priority of evangelism." You clearly remember the Sunday prayers at your home church for a certain president to win the national elections because he was in favor of getting us back to the "biblical foundations" of America. And you remember your pastor's passionate sermons on the evil of Marxism. Your understanding is coming full circle: Politics was not the question, it was right or wrong politics that mattered.

Your passion for Jesus' work and his special love for the downtrodden were viewed now as a shift to liberal agendas, and in a very short time you dropped from being the favorite missionary son of the church to having made a shameful departure from the way you were raised. Even members of the church mission committee who were your peers and buddies in school days, who encouraged you along your path to missions, took on a strange air of distance and disapproval once you returned home.

You are besieged by disillusionment regarding missionary service.

Mourn your loss—that is what it is. Mourn the death of vision, of friendships, fellowship, relationships with your pastor and coworkers. The world you once knew has passed away. It has died.

I have struggled so deeply with these losses at times that I was sure the only road to relief from the pain was pure cynicism. There is no place for tenderness and understanding. We cannot grow and retain our friendships, we cannot really make a difference in this world, there is no sure path to peace, good relationships, and fruitful service.

We must allow the process of grieving to run its course. Our deaths have been real, and to deny ourselves the honest and legitimate encounter with the evil of our experiences and the depth of our pain would be to deny ourselves the possibility of healing. It would be a sure ticket to the hell of cynics.

The fact is that our understanding of the world is now different. You see, life in Christ is not what you expected. Sweet-happy-go-lucky-to-church-and-prayer-meeting Christianity does not exist. Relationships fall apart, leaders fail you, missionaries approve of oppression, the world still goes hungry, and real estate values determine the location of your church's "ministry." There may be a place for dreams, visions, risk, and relationship once again, but your faith will have to be relearned from the foundations up. Something has been forever lost, and if we don't allow that fact to be a sure part of our new reality, all future vision will be a tormented den of our living denial. We must honestly and fully live through our death. We must weep in agony at the funeral of our Disneyland world, and we must resist the temptation to call it back from the grave.

Can there be anything merciful and gentle for us on the other side of our death? We must face this stark question in our naked vulnerability, because in time we will discover that death is the source of new life. Without the grave we live on illusions, and soon our heart will become sick.

The disciples sat stunned and disillusioned in the room above Mary's house. Three years of learning, healing, forgiving, stretching, and giving. The energy and adrenaline that flowed in those three short years could have supplied whole countries with electricity. But now it was all gone. Jesus' naked and stiff body was the emblem of their despair, confusion, and humiliation.

It's Friday.

But as a well-known speaker reminds us, Sunday's coming.

Our Sunday may be very far off, it may be around our next turn, but this you can believe, your Sunday shall come. This is the good news for those who live with the disillusionment of expectations dashed and visions defiled.

Wait for the morning, the resurrection of life. Jesus will come in your heart anew. He will breathe in it the fresh air of hope and vision once again. You will be transformed into a dignified friend of Jesus who has the inexplicable faith to go forward once again to feed the hungry, to heal the sick, to visit the prisoner, to work for reconciliation, to set free the captive, to preach the forgiveness of sins. And you will discover that you have joined a new company of people who have been raised from similar death, who have mourned similar loss.

God speaks to us through the voice of the prophet Isaiah:

> Come, all you who are thirsty,
>   come to the waters;
> and you who have no money,
>   come, buy and eat!
> Come, buy wine and milk
>   without money and without cost.
> Why spend your money on what is not bread,
>   and your labor on what does not satisfy?
> Listen, listen to me, and eat what is good,
>   and your soul will delight in the richest of fare.
> Give ear and come to me;
>   hear me, that your soul may live.
>
> —Isaiah 55:1–3

Your joy will come in the morning.

15

Our Own Bumbling

My first year out of high school I participated in a youth outreach program that involved traveling to sixty cities, where we joined local Christians in evangelistic rallies. Only twice during the year were we given the weekend off.

Nigel, who was on this program for the second year in a row, decided on a free weekend that he would like to visit his family, for he had seen very little of them in the previous year. The only problem was that the weekend was only three days long, and Nigel's family lived approximately a thousand miles away. Because we were not being paid during the year of ministry, flying was not an option—he couldn't afford a ticket. Hitchhiking, a very common means of transport for college-aged students back then, was affordable, but by the time you travel a thousand miles each way by car you have completely used up the three days.

In his quiet time this particular morning, Nigel got his message from the Lord: He would go home that weekend via "Philip's

Transport." You remember, the Lord transported Philip from the desert to the Azotus instantaneously after he baptized the eunuch.

Nigel's faith was high as a towering blue gum tree, and we all watched as he slung his pack over his back and walked down the winding farm road to a spot in the highway. There he stood, waiting for the Lord's delivery system. It was a very long day, but Nigel's faith held firm. That night he finally wrapped himself in a blanket, lay down in a storm ditch, and fell asleep, expecting to wake at home. Instead, he was met by a frightfully cold morning and day two of waiting. That night, once again he went into the rain ditch, and the next morning, he was once again awakened by the freezing weather.

Close to nightfall, Nigel lumbered his way back up the road to the camp. He was exhausted and furious. Why hadn't God come through? We, of course, were able to see the humor in the event quite immediately, and we tortured Nigel with our unrestrained laughter. It was no joke to him back then, but he and I have since laughed together quite a few times.

Sometimes our pain is a result of our own bumbling.

Unfortunately, though, it rarely involves such bizarre actions as Nigel's and such inconsequential outcomes.

If you have been badly hurt in the experience of ministry and the church, then you will know how people around you hasten to point out that you were a part of the problem. Perhaps their motivation is to help your anger and rage subside by showing that you basically have no one to blame but yourself. Such unsolicited "help" will serve to short-circuit the process of healing—anger needs the freedom to run its course—and it also burdens the poor soul who right now just needs some tender love and affection. There will be time to confront the personal failure.

Actually, very few of the miserably hurt people I know deny the contribution of their own failures to their downfall. Nearly all of them are overcome with a sense of their shortcomings and depressed at their unworthiness to fit the post of responsibility they had accepted as a trust.

Before looking at our own bumbling any further, I need to reiterate that there is pain that has absolutely no relationship to our errors. Many people are quite simply the victims of another—the junior high girl who was raped by the youth pastor, the pastor who was ungraciously dumped because of jealousies, the ministry leader who resigned because of crippling slander—and to ask them to find their own complicity in the pain is a cruel and uncompassionate deed.

What about our failures in ministry?

I think that I can identify at least two types of stumbling that have brought pain into my own life. The first, which I mentioned earlier, is simply the consequence of learning to walk. Just as a child whose incisor is forced up into the gum because of a fall on the sidewalk has to live with some discomfort for a while, we all find that following Jesus involves stumbling and its related pain. These are only the natural, nonspiritual experiences of growing up with Jesus. We don't lecture a child for catching her toe on a rock and consequently falling to the pavement; neither do we lecture Nigel. The kid will learn, and so will Nigel.

The second way I inflict pain on myself is when I try to accomplish tasks that are outside of my training, gifting, or skills. I sincerely work to meet ministry demands and to please those who are in authority over me, but I just cannot do well enough. Sometimes the consequences are minimal—for example, we didn't get a very good turnout at our church's weekend marriage retreat because the volunteer promoter had never done a brochure before, and by the time the unlovely product was off press, most people had made their weekend plans. The lesson is quite simple—next time, don't volunteer. And if the pastor asks you, say that you appreciate the gracious request, "but no thanks."

Or the consequences could be much more serious: The board fires you for lack of performance. You gave your best, but you had been too eager for the position and oversold your skills. Now you face shame, unemployment, bitterness, and spiritual dryness. There are some deeper lessons to be learned here. One, be upfront. Those who extend themselves financially and otherwise for you have the right to know the truth of your skills. If you are not sure whether you can meet their expectations, tell them what you *can* accomplish. Two, perhaps you really thought you were able to do the task. You were wrong, and the consequences you now experience are entirely disproportionate to any mischievous intent in your heart. The experience, however bitter, affords you an opportunity to reflect on your strengths and weaknesses. Intentionally avoid making new commitments where you know you cannot deliver. Work from your strengths. The Lord has gifted us in such a way that we need each other. If your failure leads you to paralysis, then the rest of us are the losers because your particular contribution is not available to us. If necessary, seek professional input to help clarify your gifting.

You need to make amends to those you have hurt or wronged through your unrealistic inventory of your skills and capabilities. You have erred. The process of healing will not be complete without this step. If it is difficult, let it take the time it needs, and pull in a couple of trusted friends to help you through the process. It is possible that you will get bogged down in guilt for having failed another. Take the freedom that Calvary and conviction offer you, and then get on with it. If the Lord seems to be telling you that restitution involves more than a verbal apology, then listen up. Every time we stifle the Spirit we are preparing the way for even greater failure. The Lord is quick to understand and forgive. We will not benefit from that mercy unless we respond to the Spirit's nudgings.

Sadly, there are times that our failures have disastrous consequences, introducing permanent loss into someone else's life. Our pain is connected to the pain felt by that person. We know that we could have chosen to live a private life—stay away from others, care only for ourselves, not risk beyond our own skin—but we chose to reach out, and in the process of reaching out we brought hell to another's world. Perhaps your experience is as devastating as that of the campus staffworker who took a vanload of college students on retreat into the mountains. He was not an experienced driver in snow, and, rather than listening to his better judgment when a storm hit, he drove on up the winding mountain road and plunged the van over a cliff on an icy curve. Two students were killed; a third still lies in hospital a year later, a complete vegetable.

The pain of telling the parents was beyond words, and then the staffworker faced them again in court, for they sued for emotional loss. There has been no reconciliation, and there cannot be hope for it.

Healing requires facing the pain you have caused others. It cannot be done alone, because if you honestly face the impact of your failure it will nearly crush you. Jesus is in the business of helping devastated persons. Lean on him, and trust the Comforter to do exactly what that title promises. Accept that you will never understand the real depth of the pain you have caused. Get as close as you are able, but don't presume to plumb the depths; that would only add to the victims' pain.

God's forgiveness makes sense only when we need to be forgiven. Sounds strange at first, but actually, I have discovered that many of us miss God's forgiveness because we don't believe we deserve it (we are right on that point). We figure we should not have failed God, and therefore we cannot go to God for forgiveness. Yet that is the very function of forgiveness: It operates on our behalf precisely because we are not capable of perfect living.

In fact, our need for God's forgiving Spirit will become all the more apparent to us the longer we live as God's children. The closer we get to the light, the more despicable our deeds and attitudes appear. We stand now in a clear contrast between what is perfect and what is fallen.

Thank God for having chosen to love us *in our imperfection* and failure. Let God's tender kindness go to work at mending your broken spirit. It is a process, and you must be patient with it.

Eventually you may find yourself motivated to reach out again, to trust the Lord to bring gentleness to other lives through you. You will have learned some lessons through earlier failures, and you will have experienced that grieving process of disillusionment—the realization that a desire to serve does not in itself qualify one to serve. There are many more ingredients to caring for others besides sincerity.

Take comfort in Scripture:

For God did not send his Son into the world to condemn the world, but to save the world through him. Whoever believes in him is not condemned.

—John 3:17–18

In repentance and rest is your salvation, in quietness and trust is your strength.

—Isaiah 30:15

The sacrifices of God are a broken spirit; a broken and contrite heart, O God, you will not despise.

—Psalm 51:17

Satan will kick you when you are down. He will convince you that you do not feel any remorse, although every indication recognizable to your friends (and normally recognizable to you) clearly states otherwise. You must rest in the knowledge that the Lord is the one who has the job of recognizing the contrite heart. Neither you nor Satan has that responsibility.

Trust in the Lord's character and, finally, join the dance of pain with others in healing who are moving out once again in the love of Jesus. It's there you will discover there is only one who is truly righteous. You and the others are all the same. For some reason we have been given the privilege of blessing fellow humans with the grace of Jesus, and now, because of our difficult encounter with our own failure and mending, we will be touching others with a humility that underscores our common fallenness. Together we lean on Christ, our only hope of glory.

And indeed, one day we will be fully glorified and there will be no crying there.

PART THREE

Risking with Jesus

Face the Trauma, Feel the Laughter
The Elusive Way of Discipleship
Outside the Gate
Invitation to Intimacy
Invitation to Healing
Invitation Home
Jesus in the Cage

16

Face the Trauma,
Feel the Laughter

Are you ready for the ride?

You and I face the choice of adventure. We stand on top of a mountain. Space stretches its arms wide in front of us. Crisp, fresh air without end. Fill your lungs, run the oxygen molecules through your clogged and crowded brain—slow the pace, hesitate, and deliberately rise to the tips of your toes. Then, draw your sword. Charge savagely down the slope; swing, slash, and swipe at the demons of the air. Tumble, slide, scrape your thighs against the rocks as you heave to stab another demon rushing to escape. Crash to the foot of the mountain, and quickly jump to your feet.

"Huh! Draw your weapons, you slimy, worthless workers of ill ends!" Scatter the demons across the pasture, and scream your insults at their fading images as they scuttle back to hell. Laughing at your own insolence, collapse in the spring of living water that cools your sweaty body and fills your soul with delight.

You have been set free.

Ahead is a journey, a playground-in-wait, a new life, your life.

Michael Been, passionate leader of the band The Call, describes it in his album *Red Moon,* perhaps the most brilliant contemporary-music release of 1990.

> This is your life
> This is your world
> Beginning to end
> This is the price of heaven, our hope
> This is the time
> This is your life
>
> The push and the pull
> We give and we take
> We rise and we fall
> We bend till we break
> The future is ours
> The promise is true
> This is your life
> I've seen it before
> I've seen many times
> An impossible task cut down to size
> We stand in the breach
> We fight at the front
> This is your life
>
> A world without end
> A stroll through the fire
> The journey depends
> On the length of the wire
> We're rarely at ease
> The pressure is high
> This is your life
> So it begins
> We reach for the stars
> Lift up your voice
> Freedom is ours
> The spirit's alive
> Oh what a ride
> This is your life
>
> This is your life
> This is your world

The struggle begins
This is the price of heaven, our hope
This is your chance
This is your life

The most frightening aspect of facing our pain may be the sense that we have to return to the old life, the way things were. We were stifled and half killed by religion, so naturally we feel very little desire to become an enthusiastic member of that club.

The good news for us is that true healing will not allow us to go back to the way of religion. We don't have to fear the journey into the future out of an expectation that our past pain will be repeated. We are entering a new society as new people and, most important of all, with a new Jesus: Yes, our companion will be that untamable Messiah who sets religion on its head. He certainly has no religious expectations of us, so we are free to move forward without the weight of condemnation or bondage. For now, put aside the structures and relationships that have brought your pain. Perhaps in time, after the wounds have healed over, you will be able to return to them, but at this moment they are distractions and, more seriously, barriers on your road to recovery.

The challenge at hand will be to focus on Jesus. This is the only gateway we have to our future—in fact, the very substance of it. All things are made and held together by Jesus—he stands alone in his supremacy. One day he will stand in judgment over all of life's ills, and in his own words, "It is mine to avenge."

So take the vulnerable leap into a dynamic, living relationship with Jesus, a relationship that goes beyond the safe, academic definition of his role at Calvary. Simply giving intellectual assent to the concept of Jesus while retreating into a protective shell that guards your emotions and soul from the implications of the cross is actually to avoid the person of Jesus.

It is always risky to enter into relationships; that's just the way life is. To enter new territory with Jesus will be a risk. But the degree to which we are willing to enter a new, healthy, and nondysfunctional relationship with Jesus will become the measure of laughter we will be able to experience in the days ahead.

We are joining that dance of pain, in which the bleeding, crippled, heart-scarred, and rejected children of religion discover the rowdy beerhall where tales of victory and defeat keep patrons on the edge of their chairs in suspense. The biggest yarn-teller is Christ himself. He was known for it in his day, and the Pharisees scorned him for being in the company of rejects. They didn't know this Jesus. And we are now discovering him for the first time.

If you have ever been married, you know that the church ceremony has very little to do with the actual marriage. I met my spouse-to-be while a senior in college. I fell madly in love with Sherrie and could not imagine life without her. As good fortune would have it, Sherrie was reached by my persistence, and we decided to pledge our entire lives to each other. Why not? We were both mature twenty-one-year-olds; we could make lifelong decisions based on rational love.

We went through premarital counseling, and I recall my amusement as dear Dr. Small cautioned us to understand the hazards of relationship, the need to serve and cherish each other at all times. Was he crazy? I wondered. This guy is behaving as though I had to be convinced to care for Sherrie—love of my life, princess of the world.

I didn't hear a word at the wedding ceremony, and off we dove into marital bliss.

We have just celebrated our eleventh year together and deeply desire each other's company. We are good friends and look forward, God willing, to several more decades together. But it has not been as we envisioned. Strong marriages require hard, gutsy work.

We have all heard the story of the husband who protests in disbelief when his wife doubts his love for her: "But honey, I told you I loved you when I married you." We laugh because we think he's a royal jerk. And we laugh because our own foolish youthful notions are uncovered by the story.

No, a good marriage is established every morning when we get out of bed. It is the decision *that* morning to tenderly love and nurture our husband or wife. It is a decision that is made without regard for "points earned" in previous months or weeks. If we are married, it is because we are married *today*. The vows taken at the altar take on significance only in retrospect.

I know of no healthy marriage that rests on the strength of the altar ceremony. I know dozens of Christian couples who are legally married but not married in their hearts. Their legalistic religion keeps them under the same roof (and sometimes under the same sheets), but their love is far gone. I also have friends who have never met Jesus but are really married. No legalistic vows keep them together. Rather, it's that daily resolve-of-the-heart to live for the other. Stormy arguments and disagreements are common to their communication, because they are absolutely intent on keeping clear channels between them.

If our marriages don't know what it is to have good fights, then we probably are not married beyond the paper. Perhaps we are just living under the same roof for the trade-off of security for sex and stability for housework. Or perhaps the one spouse lords it over the other and does not permit argument. Her dignity is squashed; she sits quiet to avoid the terror of upsetting his rule.

Going with Jesus is not unlike a marriage relationship. We made a commitment long ago, but the relationship just didn't turn out as the evangelist promised. It is possible to settle into the security of a doctrinal afterlife and leave the relationship no more developed than the little prayer at the altar. That may describe a legal contract, but it certainly does not describe a healthy relationship.

We are faced with the question: Do we want to risk Jesus? Do we want to know him? Are we willing to take the emotional chance—gamble, if you will—that we can engage all of our passions, hurts, frustrations, minds, gifts, and feelings and come out on the other side linked to each other as best friends? There is no other way if we want to be fully Christian.

This option does not come to us easily as we confront the trauma of our past pain. Why risk another ravaged heart? we wonder. Can we live through another set of disappointments and betrayals? Quality relationship is not going to emerge in any other context than our facing the fears head-on and deciding to risk. It is a hardnosed, daily purpose of the will and emotions, a chosen willingness to bet against the odds of past losses.

And if we don't take the gamble, we never will know.

For some, this suggestion of gamble may be sacrilegious. God is the way of life. That's all there is to it. You believe it, you say it with your mouth, and by faith you live a good life and wait for the day of glory. For these folks, there is either a total denial of their own pain or an experience of life that has kept them free of hardship or broken relationships. They have no doubts, and they consider such to be a sign of weak theology or lack of faithfulness. Ignore them, they are poison to your system, they have no words of life to offer a trampled soul.

If we have found courage to come back to Jesus, if we have found the way through all the pain, just enough to risk once again, then we can begin to dialogue with him. We will discover that Jesus really does wait to hear the questions, to argue the facts, to hug our tired and ravaged bodies, to make account for what we perceive as his failures.

We need to be clear and specific about our disappointments— not to ensure that he will be able to hear us (he does), but to be sure *we* hear our own hurts. There are many ways we feel that we have been betrayed by God, and these hurts keep us distant. For our own sakes, these need to be central to our conversations and arguments. We must be as thorough as our emotions allow. This is fundamental to a restored relationship. Jesus asks us to bring our honest struggles to the relationship. In time we'll discover that Jesus never has betrayed us and never will.

In some ways it is like learning to walk all over again after a serious accident. The gashes have healed, but there are wounds inflicted on the bones and joints that make our bodies permanently different. We need to have courage to stand and to experiment. We need to be sensitive to the jolts of pain, adjusting old patterns to fit our new body. And eventually we walk.

There is a fundamental quality to Jesus' character that can give us comfort as we risk this new relationship: dignity. Jesus created us with dignity, believes in our dignity, and will always treat us with dignity. This is probably the most trespassed part of our character, the most devastating aspect of the pain that we have experienced at the hands of others. We were useful to them for a time. They had their plans and empires, and we were brick and mortar. When we, for some reason, no longer complemented the designs they had on their lives, we were easily discarded. Flushed down the toilet.

All slander and disregard trespasses your dignity. We are in danger of becoming beasts because of that mistreatment. C. S. Lewis, in *The Weight of Glory*, gives stark warning on this front:

> It is a serious thing to live in a society of possible gods and goddesses, to remember that the dullest and most uninteresting person you talk to may one day be a creature which, if you saw it now, you would be strongly tempted to worship, or else a horror and a corruption such as you now meet, if at all, only in a nightmare. All day long we are, in some degree, helping each other to one or the other of these destinies. It is in the light of these overwhelming possibilities, it is with the awe and circumspection proper to them, that we should conduct all our dealings with one another; all love, all friendships, all play, all politics. There are no ordinary people. You have never talked to a mere mortal. Nations, cultures, art, civilization—these are mortal, and their life is to ours as the life of a gnat. But it is immortals whom we joke with, work with, marry, snub, exploit—immortal horrors or everlasting splendors. This does not mean that we are to be perpetually solemn. We must play. But our merriment must be a serious kind—and it is, in fact, the merriest kind—which exists between people who have from the outset taken each other seriously—no flippancy, no superiority, no presumption.

We cannot let those who have abused us triumph in the final battle for our souls. Their betrayal and savage plundering of our innermost self should naturally lead to the creation of beasts. But we have the victory; we have seen the ploy for what it is, and we are refusing to be destroyed.

Jesus comes to us in absolute dignity. He created us and finds any violation of our beauty a blasphemy against himself. He will never cross our dignity. If we are willing to risk this Jesus, then we are ready to proceed. Yes, this is our life, the choice is ours. The struggle begins, and we are the ones who decide to move forward.

Jesus risked for us at Calvary. No guarantees were available to him that anyone would respond to the act of love. But he took the chance anyway, and his reward is a band of people who are loved in the dignity of one who understands shame, betrayal, and abandonment. He will not turn away.

If you can see your way ahead with Jesus, your reward will be the sumptuous feast of life itself.

17

The Elusive Way of Discipleship

Some of the simplest tasks can turn into a circus of events.

Recently my friend Riciero helped me fix my car. He determined that all I needed was a thermostat, so, thankful for a small bill of repair, we took off to the parts store in a car he borrowed from his boss. Cruising toward Main Street, we smelled a fire. It was clearly getting closer, and we kept looking out the windows to spot the source. "It's weird," said Riciero, "smells like a paper fire." Soon the smoke became fairly dense, and as we turned onto Main Street, I swung to look out the back window in the direction of the smell. Smoke was pouring through the rear speaker holes into the back seat.

"*We're* on fire!" I shouted to Riciero.

He stomped on the brakes, car in the middle of the road, and I threw the door open for our escape. Just then Riciero shifted into reverse to get the car closer to the curb. The car jolted backward, and my open door crunched into the sidewalk, halting the vehicle and demolishing the door.

"It's full of gasoline," Riciero yelled. "We've got to put the fire out or the whole car will explode!"

Either it was our nerves or it was a bum lock, but we couldn't get the trunk to open. With the flames licking their way through the speaker holes now, these desperados took a long screwdriver from the front seat and smashed in the lock. We sprang the trunk, and both of us grabbed the flaming materials and threw them all over Main Street, stomping them out as we went along. Finally we were slapping the remaining flames in the trunk, till all that remained was the smoldering smell of electrically induced fire.

The adrenaline was still pumping strong from the fear of being rocketed into the air from a gasoline explosion, and we collapsed to the curb, laughing at the sight of garbage strewn all over the street, cars backed up, door ruined, lock destroyed, and smoke winding its way into the air from the left rear light assembly. We waved to the audience and tied down the trunk, and I held the door closed as we completed our routine twelve-dollar errand without further interruption.

Another average day of car mechanics for me.

Life is more full of surprises than not. In my experience, Chevy Chase's experience in National Lampoon's *Christmas Vacation* is more believable than the Disneyland versions of the dreamy season.

Our journey with God is no simple A-to-B proposition. There is a saying regarding sin, for example, cautioning that if you do not want to end up at a certain destination, don't take the train that will get you there. Sounds pretty solid. But then life is more like a maze than a simple diagram.

Take another routine experience. I had to travel to a very important business meeting in Boston from my home in Los Angeles. Sherrie, my spouse, was away in Israel, so I carefully planned out the care of our kids in my absence. On the morning of the 6:30 A.M. departure, I dropped off all three children at a friend's house in Anaheim at 4:30 A.M. That gave me two hours for the remaining forty-five-minute drive to the airport. I am not usually this careful—I enjoy living on the edge—but this time I wasn't taking any risks, because I could not afford to miss that evening's meeting.

But then, of course, one cannot control all the variables. That morning, during peak rush-hour traffic, the city of Los Angeles started a construction project on the stretch of freeway between Anaheim and the airport. Makes sense in L.A.

I found myself involuntarily parked for more than an hour while the construction crew did whatever important couldn't-wait-till-8:00-P.M. task was complete. Finally, I was able to inch off to the nearest exit and snake my way through a web of side streets to the airport. I pulled up to the white curb, which a computer recording dutifully reminded me was "for passenger loading and unloading only," and I shot my way to the front of the ticketing line: 6:28 A.M.

"Sorry, sir, the gate has been closed; we'll be happy to book you on the next available flight." That was two hours later and would have been too late for the meeting in Boston. All this good planning gone to waste.

Not willing to give up so easily, I dashed through security up to my gate. Sure enough, it was closed. An airline official stood nearby, so I gave him the freeway sob story, but he was not moved. Something about "federal regulations," he told me. I explained to him in very civil terms that this was important to my job. Nothing moved this robot. Finally I dropped to my knees, held my prayer-clasped hands up to his highness, and said that my very job security was dependent on his understanding and mercy.

They don't have a standard comeback for that in the "How to Be Tough" section of the employee training manual. He pushed the security-code combination and took my ticket stub. His big hand half shoved me through the door, and his parting shot was that I should plan better for the traffic.

I plopped into my seat and thanked God for sovereign intervention.

The plane arrived in Boston almost an hour early. I deplaned and went to the ticket counter to inquire regarding the bus service to downtown Boston. "That would be a long ride, honey," the woman cautioned.

"That's all right, the plane got here an hour early, and besides, I've done that bus trip before. I'll get to my business meeting in plenty of time tonight," I told her.

She didn't think so. In her estimation it would be a good twelve-hour ride.

"Your freeway traffic in Boston must be as bad as L.A.'s," I bantered back.

"Boston?" she returned. "Son, this is Atlanta."

Couldn't be. I showed her my ticket stub. "Eastern Airlines?" she questioned again. "This is the Delta terminal."

The conversation about buses was beginning to make terribly good sense. The wrong airline to the wrong city. She checked for the next available flight to Boston, and sure enough, I faced another two-hour wait. "Intolerable," I told her. "I have a business meeting tonight that I cannot miss. Put me on another airline."

She became defensive and started to accuse me of intentionally flying to Atlanta. There was only one recourse left—the ugly American. I sinfully indulged. "I can't believe you people would do this to me," I complained, raising my voice ("you people" is a wonderful phrase in these situations). "I am innocently led onto the wrong airline going to the wrong city, by your gatekeeper. Now I am about to miss my meeting, and you are blaming me for your errors?"

Shouting fights are not good for public image. A manager stepped in and quickly resolved the problem by discovering a plane that was about to leave the gate for Boston. There was one seat open on the aircraft, and they would be happy to hold the plane while I was being ushered over to the gate. The seat was in the first-class section. Don't you just love those little cheese tidbits and fancy crab salads they give the people up front?

Although circuitously, I made it to my meeting on time, and with extra pampering at that. (By the way, I found out upon my return to L.A. that it is cheaper to leave your car in the white zone and pay the towing fee if you plan to be out of town more than four nights. And security parks your car for you.)

These car-repair errands and plane trips seem to have more in common with my walk with the Lord than the simple steps from A to B to C that so much Christian literature describes. I am not helped by the books that offer themselves as "The Path to Spiritual Growth" or the "Ten Basic Steps to Christian Maturity." I end up feeling bound, burdened, and guilt-laden by their easy formulas that don't match my apparently complicated life. It's like insisting that if we just gas, oil, and wash the car regularly, all will go well. I have seen quite a few clean, full-up cars badly mangled on the freeway.

In my experience, the way of discipleship is not very easy to grasp. There is no map. It is ambiguous, ill-defined, and full of surprises. The title on the rough draft of my life's discipleship story is "Why Do I Keep Getting Where I'm Not Going?" Those who are packaging our life with Jesus as anything less complicated are doing us a disservice, setting us up for sure failure and disappointment.

The sense of failure and disappointment is particularly penetrating when we are dealing with the pain of religion.

We ask ourselves whether a more balanced life of Bible reading, prayer, fasting, Scripture memory, and church attendance could have prevented our calamity. We are told that we can come to Jesus with confidence and trust, that he will give what we need—there is no need to hold back. So we come to the Lord, but rather than taking a lovely stroll through a rose garden, we end up lost in downtown L.A.

It is critical for our spiritual health that we be set free from these legalistic and lifeless forms of spirituality. There is no value to these disciplines *apart* from their integral weaving into the details of our complex and painful attempts to follow Jesus. The Scriptures are clear that we do not benefit from a mere academic reflection on or familiarity with the Word. The Scripture is useless to us aside from the application of faith. The Word is a *living* sword; it does not act apart from the heart that is calling for the moment-by-moment miraculous intervention of the Lord to sustain one in all avenues of living in this world.

The Word, in this way, is an unfathomable treasure chest of the riches of God for us. We go to the Word and there discover the call to go into the world. We go to the world, and there we face such lostness and desperate need that we are forced back to the Word. There we discover anew that God loves the downtrodden, that God's grace is sufficient for every hardship, and it thrusts us back out to the world, newly armed with love and understanding. The world pierces us with new questions, and once again we are forced to exercise by faith what we have learned in the Word. As we do this, we travel deeper into the world's and our own pain and once again are drawn back to the Word.

This is a spiral that will take us deeper and deeper into the treasure chest.

We need to be keenly aware of the danger of spiritual disciplines aside from the messy exercise of faith. Joe Christian has a daily discipline of quiet times, complete with an elaborate log of all the Lord has taught him through each day's session. I am never able to have a conversation without his managing to insert the appropriate verse of the day and back it up with quotes from the latest three Christian authors on the same subject. This has been his pattern for the several years I have known him.

He's an infant, nonetheless.

His time in the Word and prayer has been more a protected way of life than an exercise of faith. He has been able to rest in the fact that his routine is scrupulous. His security is his habit rather than his struggle to live by faith.

God is busy weaving our life story to the degree that we are willing to participate in the process. Each weaving is a superbly distinctive masterpiece. We are each a fingerprint, if you will, a unique snowflake that is crafted through our journey of faith. We are active partners in a spiritual sojourn that is fiercely rooted in the world's soil. We are not a machine that receives regular maintenance and refueling and then, like a clock, is wound up to run by itself for a little while. No, we are each a living mystery that speaks of the wonder of God-with-us—the visible display of the incarnation, that ultimate meeting point of the Spirit and the flesh. Each day is a new definition of that marriage, a relationship whose health is entirely dependent on the degree to which we insist on being actively married to Christ.

The so-called disciplines of the faith take on a new dimension and function in this light. Reading the Word regularly can become a means to reflect on the events of our lives, to bring deeper resources to our active relationship with God. We may for a time find benefit in a daily reading of new passages, or we may, from time to time, retreat into one phrase and carry that with us for a long time. For example, you may get caught on the majesty of 1 John 1:1, "That which . . . we have seen with our eyes, . . . and our hands have touched—this we proclaim. . . ." The wonder of touching the everlasting with our hands. Every day for three months you are captivated by that testimony of the sovereign. You do not deviate from it. And you find yourself holding the hand of a little child in the marketplace, turning a leaf in your palm as you sit among others that have just fallen, or feeling the snow perch on your extended tongue.

That which we have *touched*.

The Word is alive in you, and you agree with all your heart that if you were to become silent, the leaves and snowflakes would join in a marvelous chorus of praise.

Sometimes we are best served with a season of daily readings; at other times we do well to set aside one day each month for un-interrupted playing in the treasure chest. Whatever helps us in the tangle of faith alive in the world is what becomes our aid to spiri-tual development. The one serves the other, and the means are entirely disposable.

The true disciplines of our spiritual life are not the exercises of prayer and reading and fasting and going to church—no, they are the exercises of living by faith, hope, and love, the implementa-tion of these in a fashion that forever alters both ourselves and the world. Rather than being burdened with more rules for Christian living, we are drinking from the fountain of living water, we are eating our fill of bread, we are wrestling with the power of dark-ness by rejecting its prescriptions for "godly" living. The Pharisees knew the art of spiritual disciplines, yet they failed to worship the one their disciplines were meant to point toward when he walked into their very midst.

Activists, too, have to relearn the disciplines. Too often for them the Word has been a guidebook into all the nations. Each verse has to be the pregnant anticipation of call-up orders to "go." We leave our quiet times disappointed if we do not find another di-mension of the mandate to reach all the world. We are unable to understand the selfish reading of Scripture that would simply leave us enamored with the splendor of God. Our crutch for our self-worth has become our task, and so now we use the Word to boost our approval ratings before God rather than simply delighting in Jesus.

I know, I've been in that parched land.

Jesus is inviting you and me to join him in the writing of our stories. It takes courage to venture out where once we were badgered by the keepers of the temple, but we can have confidence that he is trustworthy, is not impressed by religion, and in fact "learned obedience" himself through the exercise of faith. Contrary to a fatalistic view of life, not even Jesus' earthly existence was recorded in the history of time until he went through with it, because, you see, his life could have ended differently. Thus his triumphant scream, "It is finished!"

Jesus has lived his story, and he is inviting us to count on him in our adventure of discipleship. There is no arena of life in which he has not had to struggle. He is offering us his partnership. Paul said, "I have fought the good fight, I have run the race." In other words, "It is finished." For Paul it was in prison, for Jesus it was on the cross. For most Christian discipleship leaders, it never seems to get further than the office building.

18

Outside the Gate

When we have been hurt by the structures of religion, we will naturally consider elements such as the Bible, prayer, church, and hymns accomplices to our pain. Whether or not they actually were is not the point for us right now. They had that perceived role, and for that reason we may find them unapproachable. We may discover that we have to walk away from some of those elements for a time inasmuch as they keep us from Jesus. Some of them will come back to our lives by Jesus' grace, but it is good to let him bring them back rather than being guided by our damaged sense of guilt and propriety.

And, in fact, in time we will gladly receive them back, because they are gifts from the Lord in our journey to his heart.

We may discover during a time like this that our previous forms of discipleship shut down our senses to other avenues of going deeper with Jesus. Perhaps we were using just a very small part of our God-given eyesight because we didn't sense the need to encounter God in any way beyond our previous experience. And we will discover that our former categories shut us away from many of the people of God because our eyes had been trained to see only a very small slice of God's family.

Just go ahead and begin somewhere. Use your imagination. Use it without being confined to the categories by which we have been trained to meet God. Try heaven, for example. I grew up thinking that heaven is the most boring spot conceivable, proved simply by the fact that we are going to be confined to singing in a choir for billions of years. What's more, the music we sing is going to be a mix of Bach and Ralph Carmichael. For me this represents a sure purgatory. What a bad joke to pull on me: My parents couldn't get me to listen to that stuff, so God is going to force it on me for all eternity. What's worse, my parents will be looking on proudly as their son, dressed in wings, sings the music of God, finally redeemed from the ways of the world, purged from his love of the devil's beat.

Well, just how many varieties of Bach can you sing over a couple billion years and continue to put on a face that suggests you are enjoying this heaven thing?

Okay, rewind the eternal tape: Enter Gordon, called into heaven via an untimely road accident. Meeting me at the gate is the angel Gabriel. He tells me that there is quite a lineup of people to meet with God due to the combination of an earthquake and a regional conflict in the Middle East. A million or so people are waiting to meet their Maker. Would I like to join him for a jam session? he asks.

Would I? Cowabunga!

Gabe takes me via vapor-astral projection to a distant valley, luxuriously green, about twenty acres in size. It bears a very eerie similarity to another patch of grass in a little place called Woodstock. On either side of the vast field is a million-watt speaker. Smack in the middle, on a stand, is a Les Paul lead guitar. Gabe walks me toward it, and I experience a sudden rush with the thought that I am finally going to play my favorite leads without error. We both climb up to the platform, and to my surprise, Gabe puts the strap around his wing and tunes up. He does a most sensational version of Led Zepplin; the sound reverberates through the platform to my feet and then chases all the way up my legs and my spine and settles in my skull.

Just when I'm beginning to think I have actually reached *heaven*, Gabe gives a mischievous smile and asks if I want to become the very strings of his Les Paul. He takes off on a furious rendition of my favorite Pink Floyd sounds and I, instead of having the pleasure of playing my most wanted leads, *become* the leads. I am fiercely and rapturously sent up and down the neck of that guitar, separated through the speaker system, and then vaporized and blasted into all eternity. And then I'm brought back together for a few rounds of Jimi Hendrix. Barry Manilow had no idea what he was talking about when he sang in '75, "I am music!"

Yes, my mind has taken me there.

And why not? The Scripture says that no eye has seen, no ear has heard, no mind has even been able to imagine the outrageous wonders God has prepared for us in heaven. I'm trying though, and it refreshes my soul to think that the same God who used divine creativity to paint this incredible masterpiece called Earth is busy designing ways to make sure that heaven is a place where there are pleasures evermore.

Music is a glorious creation; it's the very language of the soul and as such will take us places where words alone are not able. For a week I may listen every day to Ladysmith Black Mambazo's version of "Leaning on the Everlasting Arms," and every morning the next week I may revel in Bob Dylan's "Ring Them Bells." Sometimes my last waking hour is spent with earphones at full throttle to the entire recording of *Red Moon* or Handel's *Messiah*. At times I breathe in the spring air and run through the daisy fields of Pachelbel's *Canon in D Minor*.

I'm a part of the generation that was scolded for bringing everything bad into the older generation's world—you know, drugs, music, sex, and so on. Apparently some people are heretical enough to think that it was the baby boomers who ushered in the real impact of the Fall. We consistently suffered the denial, via the church, of our generation's poetry and soul language. The Beatles called passionately for a better world, and the church, instead of agreeing with the basic cry of our poets, instructed us to burn their albums.

Yes, we say we want a revolution, a changed world where people love each other and don't kill for territorial gain or to save face, where instead of living greedy lives we feed the hungry, where instead of oppressing other ethnics we reach out in unity. Why should we have been condemned for singing such words of peace?

By far the most important song of our generation was John Lennon's "Imagine." His profound call for an end to religion was exactly Jesus' message to the Pharisees. Our church expected us to be horrified that someone would plead for an end to killing in the name of religion. Why not? Hitler killed millions in that name. So did Khomeini. The Crusades did their share.

If God stirs in you a passion to love and live with integrity, through means that are outside the gates of religion, be thankful for the gift. There will always be those who find evil in your means of touching God, but they also have trouble with your politics, your hair, your clothes, and your friends. Be free. These expressions have a way of leading us to Christ, where religion is powerless to touch our souls.

There are so many other ways by which we can explore the wonder of God without being bound to the structures that took us from God. Watch the movie *Children of a Lesser God,* or *The Mission.* Read Ralph Ellison's *Invisible Man* or Annie Dillard's *Pilgrim at Tinker Creek.* Try to design seventy-seven individual snowflakes, and then count the real ones as they fall outside. How long did it take you to see ten thousand of them? How many millions do you suppose fell in the backyard during the last twelve minutes? Each individual snowflake is being perfectly crafted faster than we can count them.

Talking about creativity, did you ever think about God designing sex? Really, give it a try.

Here the three of them, in their design studio, are watching a holographic couple engage in the most intimate encounter known to humanity. Are you crazy enough to think Hollywood created that? No, the three of them put the thing together, and they surely must smile as they watch passion and abandon meet tenderness and the inner reaches of the heart. And they must laugh at the sight of two grown adults lost in hyperspace. What sort of God put that together? No doubt some fuddy-duddies want to make the case that such frolicking is part of the degenerative evolutionary process. I disagree. It points me to a lighthearted, humorous, and exceedingly sensitive Being who wants me to know something of the divine character. Spend a Sunday morning thinking through that one instead of going to church. Better still if you have a spouse to share the "meditation" with you.

Outside the gate.

Sometimes our religious training might prevent us from exploring God outside the normal avenues. Certain items have been labeled "dirty," and we fear that we are being unholy by trespassing what are no more than church rules. Obviously the Bible has standards. But we have created human standards that imprison us as we attempt to reach God. The apostle Peter is an example of a very godly man, a pillar of the church, one who personally walked with God, who had to discover the power that tradition has in denying us access to all of God's creation. His strict Jewish training had taught him to say no to certain beasts. In a dream God had to instruct him to put aside all that training and accept that nothing the Lord created is unclean. Those who would control you have long lists of what you may not touch.

Jesus has a way of shortening that list.

Not to say that this freedom is easy. We have to develop our own new sensitivities and conscience. Peter was so defiled by his religion that he thought certain persons were too defiled for the gospel. Religion taught him racism, but God provided the mercy to free him from it. Our categories are just as pitiful as Peter's.

This leads to another fundamental way we will have to go outside the gates of religion to discover Jesus.

Where I grew up in South Africa, Soweto was just three miles away. The government's brilliant though insidious system of apartheid had set up black settlements so that it was almost impossible for whites to catch a glimpse of black conditions. Add to that the restriction of free press, and you have a situation in which any crime can be committed against the black person and go unchallenged. In purely political terms it succeeded, because the government could tell us that all blacks were basically happy with their lives under the white regime. No one could adequately challenge that view in the press, so the grand design of apartheid moved forward.

Of course there always were a few blacks who were vocal enough to be heard, to communicate the message that in fact their living conditions were inexcusably inhumane. But the government, cloaked in its religious guise, was able to reassure us that such voices were nothing more than the leaders of communist-inspired terrorists. We were glad to be put at ease with such an obvious explanation.

But what about all those other emerging voices that were critical of the government and clear on the horrible conditions of the blacks—voices that didn't come from some radical political corner, but from the black Christian leadership? There was only one way to deal with them. The government reassured us that they, too, were nothing more than communists in clerical garb.

The fundamental strategy being employed, of course, was simply to say that any contrary voice was terrorist in origin. We were then effectively trained to shut out anyone with an opinion that diverged from the government line. Stay away from Soweto, from militant black leaders, and from black pastors who disagree with the missionaries and government. They are bad news for the country and will defile you with their ideas. Clearly, this sort of training disciples us in the art of arrogance and the inability to listen. We are not interested in knowing anything about others, because we have already been told what they are like.

If you were a white Christian leader and spoke out against the oppression, you were called a liberal and the communist label was slapped on your organization—as with the South African Council of Churches, the religious association most committed to justice for all ethnic groups. Anyone belonging to the SACC was automatically irrelevant to evangelicals and fundamentalists. If you wanted to discredit someone's ideas in those circles, just mention that you heard he or she had attended an SACC event. I have brochures from Christian groups showing photos of certain people at SACC events, with captions like "Yoked to the Devil." Such accusations did not seem particularly outlandish to us well-trained folk.

I am fortunate enough to have parents who helped me venture behind the color curtain of apartheid—to begin to meet and listen to people who all these years had been labeled without any chance for defense (but then who gives a political enemy equal air time?). To my surprise, I discovered that I wanted to be one of them, that many of my own longings for integrity and justice were already being expressed in their discipleship. I found in them deep spiritual resources that I had never experienced in all my white living. I began to learn from them. My life was profoundly enriched as these men and women opened up truths that had been hidden to me. They led me to a new encounter with Jesus that has altogether altered my vision of the Christian life. I am indebted to them for the rest of my days on earth.

To be sure, my going behind the curtain brought down on my head the wrath of many who felt I was betraying the faith (to be read "politics and family tradition"), but that is part of the price for venturing outside the camp.

The benefits, of course, far outweigh the rejection. We discover that Christians are everywhere—the pentecostals, the ecumenics, the Baptists, the Catholics, and the Episcopalians. All this time we had been robbed of the traditions and the wealth of spirituality that others could bring to our experience of Christ. Our little corner on the truth was little indeed. All along we thought we had been protecting the purity of faith, but actually we were protecting certain political and economic ideas. You ought to resent such abuse at the hands of leaders.

Imagine there's no religion. . . .

In the end we discover that Jesus went outside the gate himself. The religious leaders did not appreciate his expressions of faith, his insistence on breaking the rules. Remember how it happened?

> The high priest carries the blood of animals into the Most Holy Place as a sin offering, but the bodies are burned outside the camp. And so Jesus also suffered outside the city gate to make the people holy through his own blood.
> Let us, then, go to him outside the camp, bearing the disgrace he bore. For here we do not have an enduring city, but we are looking for the city that is to come.
>
> —Hebrews 13:11–14

And so, you too will bear disgrace: the disapproval of religious people who look askance at your seeking Jesus outside the gate. Love yourself enough to choose freedom. When you find the Son, you shall be free indeed, and then you will understand that there is no price too high to pay for such a treasure.

19

Invitation to Intimacy

Arise, come, my darling;
my beautiful one, come with me.
—Solomon

The Beatles were right to tell us that "all you need is love." The church of the sixties was unfortunately so hung up on the strange and radical ways of the younger generation that it missed the simple and profound cry for love. This idea was not created by a hippie band of drug-filled minds plugged into an amp—it is the clearest and deepest message of the gospel. No matter what, nothing can separate us from the love of God. All the ways of the Lord are loving. I have loved you with an everlasting kindness.

The error was not in the Beatles' call for love, no matter how vague or even mistaken their understanding of true love was; the error was ours for not coming to stand with them in absolute agreement with the total sufficiency of love. What a bridge we could have extended to their partial view of love. But instead we burned the flimsy bridge that was already in place.

A seventies musical theologian, Olivia Newton John, also expressed an angle of that call: "Hopelessly devoted to you," she crooned, and nothing could be closer to the truth of what Jesus desires for us in relationship to him.

Arise, come, come my darling; my beautiful one, come with me!

Later in this Song of Solomon the lover talks to the beloved:

> How beautiful you are and how pleasing,
> O love, with your delights!
> Your stature is like that of the palm,
> and your breasts like clusters of fruit.
> I said, "I will climb the palm tree;
> I will take hold of its fruit."
> May your breasts be like the clusters of the vine,
> the fragrance of your breath like apples,
> and your mouth like the best wine.

The beloved replies:

> May the wine go straight to my lover,
> flowing gently over lips and teeth.
> I belong to my lover,
> and his desire is for me.
> Come, my lover, let us go to the countryside,
> let us spend the night in the villages.
> Let us go early to the vineyards
> to see if the vines have budded,
> if their blossoms have opened,
> and if the pomegranates are in bloom—
> there I will give you my love.
>
> —Song of Songs 7:6–12

Yes, the Lord is inviting us to a passionate abandon. A life lost in his love, where we roam the hills and valleys of life drunk with the wine of encountering him, giddy in the anticipation of more time in privacy with him. Why should we be surprised that it would be this way? Indeed, why should it be any different?

The most profound mystery of the human existence is the passion between lovers. It is the subject of every poet, author, screenwriter, musician, historian, teenager, playwright, and therapist. No other mystery has allowed us to venture so deep in the exploration and experience of its offering, and no other mystery has remained so distant from us.

And it is this profound mystery in which you and I have the privilege to frolic.

When we have drunk its wine, when we have exhausted ourselves on its extravagant pursuit of our heart, when we have eaten of its pleasures to our fill, then we will have known the transformation of the abandoned, desperately lonely virgin into a thirst-quenched mate; then we will have known the transformation of a discarded, devastated prostitute into a tenderly fondled, admired lover; then we will have known the transformation of an abused, frightened teenager into a giving, receiving partner in true mature intimacy.

Religious leaders are frightened by the apparently frivolous, uncontrollable territory of passionate abandon. We must have order, we must have rules, we must have doctrines that let intellect direct the heart.

Yes, we must risk. We must turn our backs on the pitiful expressions of doctrinal love extended to us by the religious rulers as we enter the wild abandon of relationship with Jesus, where we have to trust him for the outcome, where we are no longer in control.

We fear this plunge, ultimately, I believe, because it stirs our deepest hurts—there is no greater pain than the trespassing of the heart. We have been sorely abused, we have put a wall about our vulnerable private territory, and we hesitate to enter the undefined territory of love again.

Jesus invites us to love him and to be loved tenderly by him. It's a risk that we have to choose, and it is the only road to the heart of the gospel.

We may seek to fulfill our need for that love with society's options, allowing ourselves to become seduced by the rewards of fulfillment—work hard, focus on your talents, accomplish tasks that have a definite endpoint. Or we are seduced by significance— gain notoriety, recognition, status; live your life so that others will notice you and place titles on your door and hand out awards. We may be seduced by the comfort offered us by the American dream—live in just the right house or neighborhood; guard your recreation and time to fit the patterns of *Dallas* or *L.A. Law*. We find comfort in these pursuits, and so we accept them as partners. Or on a more subtle level, we pursue friendships as the substitute for passionate abandon with Jesus—the perfect mate, next-door neighbor, lover, children, committees, professional associations. As long as any of them replace the love of Jesus, we will not be satisfied.

We are misguided to think it is only the non-Christian who has this problem. The Christian who is seduced by these prostitutes, if you will, may go through life with the security of a doctrinal relationship with Christ but will never know the ardent relationship with Jesus for which we were all created. We have become so removed from the possibility of this love that we don't even know we are missing it. We long for the images offered by Hollywood, or we say "Bah humbug" because we have been embittered by the disappointment of substitute loves.

Jesus says, "Come here, my love," and he does not disappoint.

Coming into this love relationship after being hurt in the pursuit of an activist lifestyle can seem almost impossible, because many activists have equated their service to God with loving God. And so there is an implied contract: If we show our love with our deeds, and in fact if we do deeds that go far beyond what others would expect of a committed Christian, then all will go well for us. Along comes the pain, and we feel betrayed—"after all we did for him." Unfortunately, we did not realize that laboring for acceptance is another form of seduction. Some mission organizations, for example, define our worth by whether or not we are plugged into God's overall purposes: "Live with meaning," they tell us. "Get with the program of God." So we try to win the affections of God through our labors.

But God's love is too genuine to be reduced to our labors. There is no purpose of God that can be matched to our love with God.

For the activist, as for the abused child, intimacy can be a very threatening prospect. It is much safer to hide in the world of achieving and meeting goals—gaining self-worth through labors. We are unable to accept that we are quite simply and unarguably loved by God. We have, as activists, accepted an untrue picture of God—a taskmaster whose only real concern after making sure we escape his hell-bent wrath is to make us work for him. So our value is measured by how much God can *use* us. My spouse appropriately labels this aberrant view a "theology of exploitation": God made us in order to use us, and that is all that gives us worth. The truth is, any work done for the kingdom outside the context of love is abusive and is a form of exploitation.

The religious leaders would want to seduce you with the idea that you can gain significance before God, just as a child's athletic performance can gain a parent's approval, but that is simply another of religion's chains. Part of the challenge you face as a former exploited activist is to trust Jesus enough to let yourself go, to fall into his magnificent love.

Yes, you must abandon yourself.

Ultimately, God's love is our only possession. Our home may burn down, our spouse may leave us, an accident tonight may take our precious children from us, a rumor mill may rob us of our public position, a stock-market crash may deplete our wealth. But nothing can take God's love from us.

The Levites in the Old Testament had the duties of caring for the temple, assisting the other Israelites in their confessions and celebrations, and pointing the whole nation toward Yahweh. They were not permitted to own homes, animals, clothes, food—anything. They received all they needed through the offerings of the people they served. God gave them explicit instructions: You are to have no possession except the love of God. In reality, that is our only possession. Everything else is a passing mist.

The Scriptures tell us that now *we* are the royal priesthood. We have replaced the Levites in the duties of caring for others, of pointing them to Yahweh. And our only real possession, the only item that is not ultimately vulnerable to this world—including the religious leaders—is the love of God. No one can take it from you, and nothing is capable of replacing it.

Passionate abandon.

Our word "fanatic" comes from the Levites. In New Testament days the Levites were so enamored with the things of God that they never left the temple. The word *fanaticus*, a Latin term, was pinned on them; basically, it meant one who is always at the temple or in the presence of God.

It is not possible to become too enamored with God. You and I are invited to become intimate with Jesus, to be loved as we've never been loved before. And to become vulnerable as we have never been before. Here we will discover the rapture of a heart that has become a symphony, here we will discover a mystery that is not defined in words or on the Hollywood screen. Here we will enter that place of tenderness, retreat into the arms of the lover after another tortuous encounter with those who would lord it over us. And this love surpasses all loves.

Paul wishes it for us:

> I pray that out of his glorious riches he may strengthen you with power through his Spirit in your inner being, so that Christ may dwell in your hearts through faith.
> And I pray that you, being rooted and established in love, may have power, together with all the saints, to grasp how wide and long and high and deep is the love of Christ, and to know this love that surpasses knowledge—that you may be filled to the measure of all the fullness of God.
> Now to him who is able to do immeasurably more than all we ask or imagine, according to his power that is at work within us. . . .
> —Ephesians 3:16–20

It's all that matters, it's worth the risk, and we will discover that his love is supremely beyond our wildest hopes. Jesus is passionate, absolutely sufficient, and he is inviting us on this intimate journey of love.

20

Invitation to Healing

We must be clear that if we come to Jesus in a vulnerable, intimate affair of the heart, it does not mean that we will suddenly experience supernatural healing. We have discussed in previous chapters all the sorts of pain that we live with due to the abuses of religion. And we mentioned that some pains are like ghost pains—they remain with us to death.

There is a certain tension that we have to live with. That is just the way the world is. We can never expect total healing in this life—though that day will come—but we can expect to survive the pain, the cruel onslaughts, the wicked encounters with evil, and to get on with our lives in a way that gives the lie to those who would work evil against us. Not only will we survive, but we will even discover that we can thrive.

The most amazing healing that Jesus brings is a friend who loves at all times. Jesus never will leave us. Over time, as this relationship grows, we will become deeply assured of our worth, because the very Person who created all the wonders of this earth finds us more fascinating and wonderful than the angels themselves, who are jealous of the love he pours over us. Our spirits begin to experience a rootedness that protects us from further storm—we know now that we are loved, and a soul that is confident in being loved is a healthy soul.

Healing takes time, and just as each of us is our own special kind of person, we require our own special kind of healing. But the point is that we can have hope: Healing does eventually come.

When Jesus' coming was foretold, our pain was uppermost in his mind and heart. This is how he instructed the prophet Isaiah to describe his coming:

> . . . to comfort all who mourn,
> and provide for those who grieve in Zion—
> to bestow on them a crown of beauty
> instead of ashes,
> the oil of gladness
> instead of mourning,
> and a garment of praise
> instead of a spirit of despair.
> —Isaiah 61:2–3

Jesus regularly reprimanded the religious leaders of his day for heaping more burdens on those who were hard pressed. The Israelites constantly heard the warning of Yahweh that they faced punishment if they did not take care of those among them who were hurting, in prison, dispossessed, and without mother or father.

Jesus does not increase our burdens. Instead:

Come to me, all you who are weary and burdened, and I will give you rest.
Take my yoke upon you and learn from me, for I am gentle and humble in heart [something none of the religious leaders could claim], and you will find rest for your souls.
For my yoke is easy and my burden is light.
—Matthew 11:28–30

We will discover that Jesus is the most perfect physician. Our needs, our hurts, our histories, the painful pictures imprinted on

our minds—all of these are under his excellent care. Religious leaders are not particularly concerned about your health; they are
concerned that you get with their program, they want to control
your mind and resources. In order to convince you to give in to
their dominion, they have consistently painted Jesus as being es-
sentially just like them.

And that is why it is so difficult at times to come to him—we
have been mistrained.

It is not biblically accurate to say that Christ is concerned only
with the eternal destination of our souls. He created all of us, and
he is concerned to bring his healing to every area of life. The Pharisees were so far off the track that he cunningly referred to them as
so healthy that they had no need of him. "I came as the great physician for those who are sick," he told them. "Those who do not
think they have need of a doctor will have no need of me."

We are able to rest in the fact that Jesus came expressly to heal
the sick. If you are slashed, crushed, bleeding, dying, then Jesus
invites you to his healing. His care is tender, and it is precisely
what our spirits and bodies need.

You may struggle with the fact of your own sinful failing. Be
comforted that whereas Satan would keep us bound up in condemnation, Jesus, again, comes as the loving physician to remove
the offending cancer. He does not approach us with a chain saw
and rip away at the sick parts. No, he comes to us under bright
surgical lights and deftly cuts at the tissue that would destroy us,
then nurses us back to health. He does not rush the process, he is
not on a timetable, he cares only that we become well.

And it is his compassion that stirs him to it:

> Jesus went through all the towns and villages, teaching in their syna-
> gogues, preaching the good news of the kingdom and healing every
> disease and sickness.
> When he saw the crowds, he had compassion on them, because they
> were harassed and helpless, like sheep without a shepherd.
> —Matthew 9:35–36

This is the Jesus who wants to love us today. He is inviting
you, harassed by the system—you, helpless from the crushing pain

and destructive rumors—you, abandoned on the fringes for having the wrong ideas.

I believe that no part of our recovery process takes more *courage* than the *decision* to move from the mindset of a victim of others' abuse to that of a survivor who is looking forward to a vigorous and happy life.

Our pain is a fact. The injustice of our circumstances is indisputable. I have always marveled at the stories of women who lived through the atrocities of Nazi concentration camps and then went on to live with the joy of Jesus. Rather than being mired in the hell of their experiences, they made a decision to choose to live, a decision in favor of healing. Who can point us to a greater courage?

I want to appeal to you if you are caught between the territory of a crushed life and a choice to go forward toward your healing. You are a marvelous person with dignity and immeasurable worth. You are a storehouse of priceless wonder. Please become a free person. Please unlock the door of your prison and go find the great physician who waits to heal. Please choose in your favor and come join the dance. Jesus is leading the band.

Come away and be loved. Come away and be healed.

21

Invitation Home

Jesus is the perfect lover. Jesus is the perfect physician. Jesus is also our perfect parent.

The way that we have been put together requires all three. John Perkins, inner-city activist, says that the church has been offering the world a corporation and all the while it was looking for its daddy.

We live in a very cruel age, one in which parenting is out of fashion. The rise of the latchkey kids, the generation gap, the growing number of single-parent homes, and of two-parent homes in which kids are considered an inconvenience, the increase in domestic violence: All of these make it more likely that growing up will be a negative experience rather than positive. There are not many teenagers today who will reflect upon their years at home as a secure, warm stretch of life that they'd love to repeat, and there is hardly a parent who would confidently say that fulfilling his or her role in parenting is a snap. The incredible growth of Focus on the Family, whether or not we agree with all its ideology, is testament to the fact. We are in a day when the family is in crisis.

And it is a vicious cycle of crisis, for because of the way children are being reared, they are likely to repeat their parents' patterns: The seed for tomorrow's broken homes is being sown today.

The most sickening thing I experience on my travels is listening to the tales of abuse in the home. Neglect is not enough. Parents have to add insult to neglect, and others add pain to the insult—incest, beatings, and confinement. Today's youth are an unloved generation, and their image of "God the Father" is not helped by their memories of an earthly father who ignored, abused, and belittled.

We must know that Jesus offers us release from those images. God is not demanding our performance, does not consider us an inconvenience, did not accidentally conceive, did not and does not despise us, and is not withholding affection pending our good behavior. God created us in love, and God is restless with our pain.

Late one night one of our daughters, just five years old, was suffering from a very high fever. We applied the necessary medication, but nothing seemed to help. The fever stayed constant and even climbed a little. We put her in a bath of tepid water, but that did not do much either. At about one in the morning my spouse held her in a rocking chair in the living room. Tamara asked in a dreamy voice if we would open the curtains. She stared out into the distant black and then asked, "Do you see those pretty lights on the other side? It's so beautiful." She expressed a desire to be there.

My heart twisted, and I was strangled with the fear that Tammy was about to leave us for a world that we were unable to see. Her peace as she contemplated the beauty only increased my panic. I cried and prayed for my little darling. She slipped asleep and woke an hour later, fever broken, her usually happy self. Who knows what was going on medically or spiritually, but it was clear what was going on in the parent. I love Tamara and cannot imagine losing her. Sometimes my mind will go back to the emotions of that moment, and I will again begin to cry.

Any decent parent who has had such an experience of coming close to loss knows what I am talking about. For some of my friends, loss was complete: Their eight-year-old had a high fever and while being rocked that evening simply announced that there was nothing to fear where she was going. Less than an hour later she was gone.

God lives in our pain. God, our parent, is able to weep our pain perfectly. Contrary to what some would suggest, divine perfection does not imply that God is untouched by the pain; rather, God is all the more touched. There is no hardened heart between our parent and the pain. God feels it harshly, severely, and cries for us.

This is our invitation home—to come to the severely hurting and understanding parent. Here again, our space of tenderness will be enlarged as we find God's arms folded around us, God's eyes weeping our pain. There is no scolding, condemning, or judging: God waits to hold us and cry with us.

And we must know that God is not only our Father. We—male and female—are created in God's image. That means that God is not all male, and we are robbed of some of God's parenting if we are unable to come to her, our Mother. The Scriptures are filled with feminine images of God that make this uncontestable—the mother eagle, the womb that gives birth, the mother hen that looks over Jerusalem and cries over our state: O that I could gather you under my wing as a hen would her little chicks. Every positive motherly and fatherly image of God that we can project or conceive is there for our comfort. God will not let us down: Just as God is the perfect lover and perfect physician, God cares for us as the expert parent. We have the freedom to crawl up into the arms of this wonderful person and, if we want, to suck our thumb while clinging to our blanket.

Those of us who have experienced pain at the hands of the religious establishment—whether directly in the form of physical or mental abuse, or at a distance if one of our religious heroes abandoned the faith or fell into serious sin—are left with the feeling of being orphaned. We left their religious house (or were kicked out), and now there is no place to go. We have no home.

For us there are the words of Jesus, who is tenderly disposed toward orphans. In fact, he went so far as to say through the apostle James that "true religion" is to care for the orphan and the widow. We are completely new people. Our harsh experiences have made it that way. We simply will not be able to go back to the life we knew. In our insecurity, at times we will be crazy enough to want the old life back, because at least its familiarity offers us something solid. Take heart: God waits to care for us; our new Father, our new Mother, is holding the door open. We are welcomed into the living room, by the fireplace, to the hearty meal, the warm embrace, the total security, one hundred percent acceptance.

And our place of tenderness is increased.

Cry your pain, don't fear the repercussions or the embarrassment of this parent. Your mother and father are sobbing with you.

22

Jesus in the Cage

Not long ago I went through quite a painful period of confusion, loneliness, and depression. I had to convince myself to get out of bed in the mornings, and in fact my best friend, Sherrie, took on the thankless task of "morning booter"—sometimes literally kicking my body from the horizontal plane.

I felt immobilized. All the great ideas and passion that had spurred me daily in my tasks held little influence over my tired body and weary soul. I found myself at the point of thinking that ministry just was not worth it.

It was a scary thought, because I didn't want to live with myself if I made that sort of decision. It was a lonely thought because I wasn't sure anyone would be able to appreciate the pain that prompted my sense of defeat. Sometimes I would panic as I lay on my bed, simply unable to move. I really wanted to give up, and I was terrified that I might do just that.

It was not a classic sort of burnout I was experiencing. My mind rehearsed all those indicators: I didn't suffer from the difficulty of balancing the overwhelming needs of the world with the limitations of my human frame. I had been through that routine eight years earlier and ended up spending three months on my back recuperating from the overdrive. I'm at peace with the fact that God in divine sovereignty is responsible for the world—I simply have the privilege of participating.

During college days the idea of slowing down or taking a break from activism had seemed too selfish, considering the fact that some people would be passing into eternity that night while others peacefully slept. The thought of eating square meals while others starved for just a piece of bread rendered many of my meals unappetizing. But that had all changed: I had learned the need of good sleep and had grown to understand the blessing of hearty meals that strengthened my body for the tasks at hand.

I used to believe that somehow my doing was more important than my being. God was to be seen primarily as a taskmaster. An intensely personal relationship with God was being forfeited for a sort of employer-employee relationship.

But that too had changed. My identity is no longer captive to my place of service. I take my work very seriously and personally, but it isn't the essence of who I am. I have been learning over the past few years that my significance is tied up in the person of Jesus Christ. Nothing else really counts except that he loves me and wants to spend all of eternity with me. My work in the world is simply an extension of that love relationship.

So why the burnout? Weren't all the bases covered?

Apparently not.

I felt like a discarded cigarette butt in an ashtray. Useless. Unwanted. All the good stuff sucked out of me. I was embarrassed at my groveling about, feeling no more dignity than that rudely extinguished smoldering butt.

My burnout was the result of not managing well under very painful criticism, accusations, and rejection by some close friends. I found myself all but crushed. Hounded by self-doubt and mocked by my own weaknesses, I eventually found myself lying face on the floor in a hotel room, crying like a baby.

I began to page through my Bible, hoping to find some comfort there. I read with close attention the words one activist used to describe his life: "troubled, hardships, distresses, beatings, imprisonments, riots, hard work, sleepless nights, hunger, hard pressed, perplexed, persecuted, and struck down."

"Another cigarette butt," I thought to myself. "How does it feel to be in the ashtray, Paul?" He claimed that he was not crushed by all of it. That's where we differed—I was sure I was crushed. I didn't know how to move forward, nor did I want to move forward.

I kept reading and discovered the pain of another activist, pleading with his father: "My soul is overwhelmed to the point of death." He asked that the load be taken from him, but the answer was silence. He knew he had to go the way of the cross. The pain didn't let up—instead, the agony increased until finally his pitiful abused body screamed out in earshot of curious onlookers, "My God, why have you forsaken me?" His life ended, however, with the triumphant words, "It is finished!" He persevered. He ran his race.

I began to understand. I picked up my journal and penned the following prayer: "Lord you have prepared a way for me to go and I want to walk that path unflinchingly in order that all the plans you have determined to accomplish through my little frame will see their fulfilled end. Please do with me as you desire and don't put a hold on your sovereign intentions because of my feeble heart."

Who knows exactly what happened? But in that desperate moment of total weakness I got off the floor in a strength not my own and walked out of that hotel room with a desire to go the distance with my Father.

There were no answers for the pain I was experiencing, just the miraculous ability to keep going.

I am offended by quick-fix answers to the problem of evil, formulas that suggest our need to comply with God's apparent sovereign designs to allow evil to have a prominent place in our lives. I resent the injustices of evil, its destructive work against friends and against me. I do not accept that we are the pawns of some great wager between God and Satan. I am not aware of any perversion so great as the teaching that pain (such as rape, disease, and death) was created simply to prove our allegiance to the one who created us. Such twisted thinking is the material of sadistic horror flicks.

And it is the material of those who have not accepted the evil of evil. If we as Christians claim that there is no darkness whatsoever in God, then we cannot suggest that God would commit evil against us (even if it is somehow "for our benefit").

That a good, creative, beautiful God exists is obvious to me. All of creation instructs my mind and heart with such clear facts. It is equally clear to me that evil wages a war against the marvelous creation, bringing destruction to what is good. The unspeakable suffering that we endure at the hands of the enemy of our souls only leaves me hoping that the flames of hell will burn long and hard for the devil and his workers of darkness.

There is no good answer for the question of why you and I, specifically, suffer. We are part of the harassed crowd. We don't look for the good in such ravaging. A leader in the evangelical world writes me that a missionary family lost their twelve-year-old daughter to suicide. Over dinner one night my friend asked the father how he was coping with the tragedy of loss. "No, it is not a tragedy," replied the missionary; "God has a perfect and sovereign will in this event." That parent is a victim of poor teaching. He cannot grieve his loss, he cannot shout his anger at God, and he cannot curse the darkness.

When we look to resolve the problem of evil easily, we become just as pitiful as this father.

I live with the evangelical hope of one day living where there will be no sorrow. That fact is about as important to me as anything. One day while enjoying the luxury of that bright existence I intend to ask lots of questions regarding the pain of this life. Now we see through a glass dimly, then we shall see with the precision of a perfectly reflected mirror image.

We face two equally important and undeniable truths that must become our companions for the rest of our days.

The first is that the world is an unjust, evil place. We will constantly be thrown about by the enemy's wicked designs on our lives. We cannot expect to live completely healed from past hurts; neither can we avoid the encounter with evil in the days to come.

We arise every morning within an arena of unspeakable evil, and we lie down at night heavy from battle, hoping for sleep to bring relief. There may come pain that is too difficult to face—we will know its source but won't be able to risk an honest encounter with it because we will fear total destruction. And there will be undefined pain that eats at our bodies, pain that is real to the nerves and emotions but does not reveal its source or cure.

This is not an invitation to defeat. On the contrary, it is an invitation to reality. If we can live in full awareness of reality, our defeat is less likely. We cannot be surprised by the encounter with darkness. We cannot hope to be free of it.

The second and vital point is this: We have one who lives with us in the pain. Jesus is not removed from the destruction of our souls. He lives with our pain, and his soul is tormented a thousand times a thousand with the agony of our afflictions. Yes, Jesus was a historical figure who went through the redemptive death on the cross to satisfy the legal requirements of overcoming the Fall, but that never was and never is the primary Jesus. He is the perfect God who created us in perfect love and now lives inside our pain. Our misery is his misery. He lives our agony and awaits the final day of relief from this difficult journey as much as we do. The pain did not end at the cross. Nor did it begin there. It was pain that drove Jesus to the cross in the first place and pain that continues to stir him to anger and compassion over our plight.

Just as pain greets me every day, so Jesus meets me in the morning with his tenderness and healing, and every night as I lie down to rest he comforts me with the thought of his presence in the coming day.

Some have proposed the idea of a God who does not feel any pain. Divine perfection, they say, makes God incapable of being affected by our condition. Calvary was supposedly the great event that satisfied the impersonal justice of God. Such a view is skewed in its concept of perfect. If I as a parent were to model my efforts toward perfection after such an understanding, I would tell my kids that their pain does not reach me.

This is a perversion of the concept of "perfect." If anything, God's perfection is demonstrated in a vast ability to agonize for the creation. When divine anger surges up against those who are oppressing the weak and the downtrodden, it is because God still feels the pain of oppression. This is good news to those who are crushed by the powerful and arrogant. God is perfect: This means that God is unable to ignore the plight of those who suffer, unable to stop working on their behalf. Beware if you think God's ear is not bent toward the cries of the "least of these."

The profound fact of the incarnation is that God lives in pain, lives with us in our pain. We have one who understands us when we come limping and broken. If anything, rather than the void of pain being satisfied at Calvary, it was perfected—that is, God's pain was made more complete. Because of the incarnation Jesus now feels our hurts more acutely.

We do not have the answers to pain, but we do have a companion who walks with us in our pain. We do not need to resolve all of pain's questions, but in order to live through pain, we may and must take the hand of one who bears the scars of rejection, beatings, mockery, crucifixion, insults, and loneliness.

When we wake in the morning to our struggle, we will find that Jesus is right there beside us in our cage of pain.

PART FOUR

Risking with the Church

The Tentative Courtship
Friendship in the Faith
Live with Dignity
Freedom to Love:
    Returning to the Pain

23

The Tentative Courtship

Some conflicts arise out of hilarious circumstances.

In high school I participated in my church's coffee-house ministry. Part of the seventies worldwide evangelistic movement, such ministries featured rooms with free coffee and sandwiches, candlelit tables, and live contemporary music. The hope was to create an atmosphere conducive to genuine conversation with non-Christians about Jesus. The coffee-house movement was highly successful in its evangelistic goals, and in fact it was at a coffee house that I had my first experience of leading someone into a personal relationship with Jesus Christ.

One evening, our volunteer staff prayed ahead of time for the Lord to be with us and give us a particular sensitivity to the Holy Spirit. We had heard that a couple of gang members would be showing up, and we prayed for them by name.

By 9:00 P.M., the evening was going well. The dimly lit room was packed as full as we had ever seen it, and George was crooning away on his guitar with Bob Dylan numbers, providing us perfect atmosphere. My partner, Tim, a missionary kid, was across the table from me, and we smiled at each other with the satisfaction of seeing our gang member friends enjoying the environment. At one point Tim leaned across the table to speak to me against the hubbub. He didn't see it, but his large blond Afro caught fire in the candle flames. I had one simple response: Save Tim from burning alive. I frantically smashed my hands into his flaming hairdo, and Tim, who was known for his quick temper, took my actions as an unprovoked and hurtful deed. He lashed out at me, tipping the candle onto the paper tablecloth. Flames. I jumped back, but his grip on my lapel stuck. His body dragged across the table, tipped it to the floor, and took several chairs down with it. Within seconds the house of God was transformed into the scene of a brawl. Others joined in our fight, and soon most of the tables and chairs were overturned, people were hitting each other without knowing why, coffee splashed on blouses, noses bled, a window shattered, and panicked patrons scrambled over bodies to escape what they were sure was a gang fight.

Eventually the youth pastor was able to find the light switch and bring the crowd to its senses. Tim continued to scream at me for bashing in his skull, and I shouted back that I was simply trying to save his head from burning off his shoulders. A stupefied silence fell on the room as Tim and I headed for the bathroom mirror. There he saw the evidence of horribly singed hair, and our anger dissolved into cackles of delight in the bathroom as the pastor watched the evening disintegrate. Gang members filed out the door, and Tim and I, quickly restored to each other in fellowship, obediently cleaned up the mess.

I wish all Christian conflicts were resolved that easily.

The earlier part of this book provided examples of severe pain, pain that may be similar to what you are experiencing because of the church. Once we have honestly recognized our abuse at the hands of religion, you and I face a choice. We can choose to walk away from religion's structures, or we can choose to risk a new relationship with it. It is my opinion that the healthier choice, in the long term, is to risk relationship. But that risk can be engaged only in the peace of your heart.

You cannot allow yourself to be pressured into it, and you must risk only if at the same time you are able to retain your dignity. When you are ready to risk honesty and more pain, you are ready to risk the church. No earlier.

The courtship begins with identifying the hurts. Some would tempt you to trade in the integrity of facing the abuse head-on, but you must resist. Specific sins have been committed against you, and you will never be free of their influence in your life until you tag them. You must call them for what they are. Some of the pain has serious consequences that are not easily repaired. For example, slander may have resulted in the loss of a ministry that you birthed and to which you gave your life. The emotions you have experienced in connection with the loss probably include everything listed in part two of this book. Perhaps your virginity was stolen by the pastor. You will never regain it. He took it and destroyed it. Be honest with the hurts, and avoid the advice of those who would have you quickly move on from the shambles. You must dwell on the wrongs as long as your heart requires, reliving the painful moments and crying your despair that your life has been irretrievably altered.

This honest encounter will release your rage: You must let rage run its course. It is a gift from God. Picture your anger galloping like a wild horse across the open plain, hooves beating in deliberate rhythm against the cruel earth, coarse air slicing your throat open, and blood choking your airways with the disgust and suffocation you feel. Eventually you lie exhausted, far from the town, cramped from the pain of your rage, awaiting the death of your soul. Your rage was your last dignified act, and now your defeat is mocking you as you lie waiting dumbly for the final rest, ruined by your own panic.

But then, finally, you awake to the friendship of honesty. Your aching body and parched throat are there to affirm your dignity, to agree with the outrage of your heart, to reward you for the honesty of your anger. You are a wonderful person and you were trespassed. Contrary to the message of the abuser, you are not trash. And you hold your tired head high as you walk back to town, ready to live your worth.

Sometimes the rage returns. Thankfully, it does not become your companion. It is a part of the journey you must take to become a healthy person. Be careful that it does not *live* with you, but similarly, be sure not to deny its place in your healing.

Rage, of course, can be expressed in both healthy and destructive ways. Love yourself and others enough to avoid the destructive avenues—the pain you inflict on others while giving vent to your pain is going to return to haunt you. Your rage is a measure of your dignity crossed—don't heap the same abuse upon another.

I have a few friends who are very helpful soundboards for my rage. They allow me the most precise and outrageous articulation of my hurts, because they understand from their own experience of pain that a relief valve is critical for the survival of pressured souls about to explode. And I scream my rage to God. I have smashed hundreds of demons to death while chopping wood, and afterward my exhausted arms and soul have soaked in the warmth of a fire built by the labors of my rage. Similarly, entire mountain ranges have been burdened with the articulation of my pain, and they always wait patiently for my hoarse voice and drained frame to rest, finally, on a peak while they return to me the expansive grandeur of their reach as a promise of God's imminent arrival.

Some have suggested that only people hurt us—not systems. That is not accurate. Systems take on a sociological life of their own and become larger than those who run them. The system of apartheid, for example, was created by evil individuals who intended to use blacks as labor units in the pursuit of comfort. But those who inherited the controls of this system were victims of it as well, in that for a time they did not understand the truth of what they were doing—all in the name of preserving law and order. The system of apartheid has no redemptive value. It is evil. It has to be destroyed. It has no capacity for good.

Some will have to let their rage run against systems. The real heroes in the world are those who have suffered abuse in the machinery of evil systems and then emerged, with all their wounds, ready to create a system that will deliver good to people. Their vision does not end with the dismantling of structures that destroy; rather, their vision *begins* with the implementation of and cooperation with structures that will deliver justice and mercy in a very crooked and broken world.

Most of our pain, however, can be traced not to structures but to individuals, and this is where our rage must eventually take us.

We cannot set timelines for the healing process we are about to engage. We have to approach it no faster than our dignity allows; otherwise we have set ourselves up to become the victim of abuse once again. Three key transactions take place in the healing of relationships.

The first is *forgiveness*. This happens when God gives you the grace to be crucified. That is what the cross event was all about. Jesus was busy forgiving everyone who sinned against him. We want to avoid false forgiveness—this is what we do out of guilt, having had it drilled into us that we must forgive. True forgiveness is what the heart allows. It is the honest cancellation of a transgression against us. This is the most serious of human endeavors and must never be the expedient act of a Sunday school-trained soul. Forgiveness is the outcome of travail, the rehearsal of abuse, the gallop of rage, the grieving of what has been lost. Forgiveness will dawn on us like the unexpected sunrise. It will come to us as a gift, and we will dispense as much of it as we have received. Most often that is because forgiveness is related to the level of pain we have experienced. As we discover implications of our pain that we had not earlier known, we experience a new loss and consequently the need for a new forgiveness. It is as though the crime were just freshly committed.

Forgiveness comes to us a little more easily when we realize that sometimes others' treatment of us was not so much a premeditated act against us as the consequence of their own fallenness, social conditioning, or dysfunctional history. This understanding does not diminish the severity of the crime committed against us, but it does allow for an easier path toward forgiveness.

One of the gifts of this forgiveness process is the revelation of our own fallenness. We begin to see the degree to which Jesus has forgiven us, and we also begin to gain a clearer grasp on how we are in need of others' forgiveness because of our violations against them. We are able to link ourselves humbly with others and go to the cross in a united call for mercy. The things we want to do we do not. The things we do not want to do we do. And God freely forgives us all. The other gift of forgiveness is that it serves as a doorway to a fresh experience of God's love. When our act of forgiveness frees others from their prison, God's love toward us is simultaneously unchained in greater measure—not because God's love for us has now increased, but rather because we have now made available fertile, healthy soil in which that love can thrive.

One key transaction in the healing of relationships, then, is forgiveness. A second is *honest encounter*. We must decide whether we want to return to deep relationship with the one who hurt us. If the answer is yes, then we must walk the perpetrator through the dungeons of our torture. There is no other alternative. The perpetrator must live the savage encounter and scream for release from the pain as if he or she were personally experiencing it. Very few relationships can survive this honesty, so we are left to wisdom's discernment of which can. Part of the harsh consequence of the Fall is that we will not experience true reconciliation with many people, because we are not strong enough to face the pain of honesty. Our ideal, then, must not be "perfection." Rather, our ideal is to be honest in relationships as far as they are able to go (there is, in fact, quite a bit of experimentation along the way) and then to pursue these relationships further from that place of healing.

And if love does "cover a multitude of sins," this is precisely where it operates. Honest, sincere conversation has led to a certain depth of forgiveness, and now love is big enough to cancel the remainder of violations without the need of a scrupulous inventory of sins. I give thanks for how divine love has covered over, and continues to cover over, gross betrayals of God. Likewise, I am thankful for the dozens of friends whose love has canceled my sins against them at depths to which my feeble heart was too afraid to descend.

The third key transaction in healed relationships is the ongoing work of *restoration,* that cherished gift for people who have been able to make the pain known as far as the wounded soul required. The road ahead is a process of restoring trust, dignity, and laughter to the relationship. These are the true friends whom Proverbs describes as "loving at all times." There are very few such friendships, and there is little this side of heaven as precious. "Nothing kills cynicism so dead as the warm love of a friend," says (and models) my good friend Ruth. As we struggle to court the church once again, we will discover the gift of true friendship, and that will become our home and base as we venture out.

I want to mention one way in which some victims of religion are being victimized further: through so-called Christian Twelve-Step programs, modeled on the successful Alcoholics Anonymous program. Basic to the AA program is the knowledge that our destructive, repetitive choices have left us almost entirely helpless and, additionally, have brought severe pain to others' lives. The Twelve Steps help the alcoholic to accept his or her total need of intervention from a higher power and to face the pain he or she has brought to others. The Christian version is more explicit in stating our need to fully trust Jesus. We are sinners and are incapable of controlling our lives. In the program we are instructed to make a list of all those we have sinned against and then seek restitution. Actually, the Twelve-Step program is the nineties version of Bill Bright's "Four Spiritual Laws" and Bill Gothard's steps to reconciliation combined. It sets the theological record straight in terms of our sin and helplessness before God and then calls for Jesus to be on the throne of our lives, extending even to our relationships with others whom we have hurt and continue to hurt by our dysfunction. Its value in this regard is attested by thousands of Christians throughout the United States; these principles are basic, solid discipleship material beneficial to anyone going deeper with Jesus.

But the Twelve Steps in themselves are far from a healer for those who are victims of others' abuses. In fact, they end up blaming the victim. We tell the raped woman to realize that she has no control over her life and that she needs to consider all whom she has abused, seek their forgiveness, and then move forward in freedom. This is cruel treatment and sinks her further into prison. This woman needs to have her dignity affirmed, the deep love of Jesus made new to her, the violent deed against her named for what it is, control of her environment encouraged so that she does not continue to live a victim of others' abuses, forgiveness encouraged, and wholesomeness pursued.

In fact, leery as I am of lists, let me venture to systematize this just a little and call it the the Six Stages Toward Wholeness.

THE SIX STAGES TOWARD WHOLENESS

1. *Affirm Your Dignity*
   Here you want to explore the reverence with which you were made, the awe with which the angels look upon you, the pricelessness of your personhood that is measurable only by Calvary's cross. You have dignity in the very substance of who you are.

2. *Accept God's Love*
   We've discussed this some in the book already. God is the perfect parent who is restless to love us tenderly and completely. Nothing can *stop* God from loving us, nothing can *spur* God to love us—we are quite simply loved. It's the profound fact of our existence, the essence of the gospel story.

3. *Identify Your Hurts*
   We have just discussed the need to face the pain honestly, label it accurately, and run the rage necessary to be free of it.

4. *Take Charge of Your Life*
   The world remains evil, which means we will continue to experience pain and abuse. But you can interrupt the patterns that unnecessarily open you up to others' abuses. Identify those patterns and then go to God with a request for help to interrupt the harmful behaviors. Ask for strength, courage, godly character, perseverance, the Holy Spirit. Look to friends to encourage you in this break from destructive ways. You must take control of your life; if not, others will.

5. *Work for Reconciliation*
   I have just outlined that process, describing three key transactions—forgiveness, honest encounter, and restoration.

6. *Pursue a Wholesome Life*

Identify the heart of what is worth living for. Take inventory of your gifts and skills (with the help and reflection of others), and then begin to live your life with dignity. Give to the world out of your restored self, and go to bed at night with the satisfaction of a life lived in integrity, by the power of the Holy Spirit.

We want to be careful not to market the Twelve Steps to people who have no need of them or who in fact can only experience greater pain because of their misapplication.

In conclusion to this discussion, I want to highlight three words that have been a part of your experience: rebellion, parenting, and accountability. It is important to unpack their influence on our lives if we are to understand some emotions we are going to encounter in our healing.

People who don't understand *rebellion* don't understand pain.

To resist is to act honorably. It is the indication that we intend to persevere in the face of persecution, the decision to label evil as evil, and the resolve to protect ourselves from evil's repeated attempts against our souls. Rebellion, in this light, is the brave and noble deed of a dignified victim of religion who is healthy enough to accept the banishment imposed by religious subgroups.

But rebellion can be confusing, because to some, rebellion is an excuse simply to destroy, to accept no limits or guidelines in life, to break down what others have lovingly and painstakingly built up. Such rebellion has no honor—it is despicable. It is best illustrated by Satan's arrogant rebellion against God, which led to his attempts to destroy you and me—God's masterpieces of love and beauty.

Yet your rebellion against certain abusive practices and structures may be labeled as destructive simply because you have chosen dignity and truth over religion. To be labeled a rebel, in this instance, is to be told that structure and tradition are more valuable than you are. You know that is not true, so live your rebellion—or your questions, if you will—as you journey toward dignity.

The simplest solution to pain is to rebel completely against human relationship—to become the island or the rock of which Paul Simon sang. It is to withdraw entirely from the vulnerable territory of human fallenness and is best understood as self-protection. Underlying this extreme response is a lack of hope. It is the conclusion that the rewards of relationship are not as great as its risks: People will screw you if you give them half a chance. Few of us, however, withdraw entirely from the human world. Rather, there is the tendency to limit the number of people whom we trust.

When we have experienced pain at the hands of *institutions*, we are likely to withdraw from and be less trusting of organizations in general. Rebellion against the structure of the church in particular is often a consequence of negative, harmful encounters with secular structures. This orientation is helpful in understanding those of us who consider ourselves "sixties" or "seventies children." Our parents were great believers in "the company"—they grew up as AT&T became a giant and threw cable into every hamlet of America; they saw the government pull the nation out of the Depression; they saw the military machine crush Nazism; and they experienced the prosperous fifties as the reward of loyalty to the company. In contrast, my generation saw the same institutions send 55,000 of our peers to the grave for an immoral and senseless skirmish in Asia; we saw the abuse of human rights activists, who were labeled as communist and unpatriotic simply because they had enough patriotism to express their own views; we saw our president attempt to cheat his way into the White House for another term and deny every step of his criminal behavior; we saw the assassinations of John F. Kennedy and Martin Luther King, Jr. We are the first generation to live under the threat of total annihilation from nuclear weaponry created by the system, paid for by the taxpayers.

It is inaccurate and unfair to say that our generation is simply a rebellious, disrespectful generation. We have learned to be wary of structure's power, promises, and abuses. Chuck Colson, at a town meeting in Northwest Pasadena, told a small group of us that the sixties generation was guilty of shifting our culture away from the Judeo-Christian heritage of our society. He is wrong; on the contrary, we would say it was the sixties child who saw the hypocrisy of elders' claiming to be Christian yet giving their lives to structures that brought hell to earth.

Religion was used to bless the system and curse those who opposed it, and so we concluded that religion was part of the problem. We could hear our elders indignantly decry the words of John Lennon, "Imagine there's no religion," supposedly calling us to an atheistic life; we, on the other hand, echoed our amen because we saw that religion was simply an excuse to continue abuses against the human race. It was our friends who died in Vietnam, and it will be our children dying because of the nuclear bomb. Why should we be expected not to rebel against the destructive forces in our lives—including religion?

You may be living in pain precisely because of the abuses of religion against your soul. Your rebellion against those structures must first be understood as a sign of health: You are unwilling to walk back defenseless to the source of your pain and allow the abuse to continue. In time you may discover yourself once again a happy church member, but that can come only after an honest and difficult dealing with the source of your pain. Anything less would not be true fellowship and would be dysfunctional at best.

We must eventually court the church in its structural form. We cannot, in integrity, deny its capacity for good. And we cannot throw out all structural religion because of our particular negative experiences of it. But this takes time and courage—not unlike the process of mustering one's willingness to date again after a romantic relationship has ended in trauma. Healthy relationship with structure is possible, but not easy.

As we attempt our own structural responses to life, we will discover just how complicated, indeed nearly impossible, it is to treat all people kindly in the context of organization. Consequently, our empathy for others who lead structures will grow. I am pained by the amount of abuse I have been able to pile on others in the name of Christian ends. I founded and operated a ministry for more than a decade, and there are mangled bodies strewn all over the terrain we traversed—victims of my religious corporation. And yet all that pain was inflicted in the sincere attempt to serve Jesus and spread his love.

We humbly attempt to do our best, understanding that our structures are not much more than cultural, sociological phenomena, as replete with evil and as capable of evil as the hamburger house next door. Yet they also have the capacity to bring a little heaven to earth. We must live with this tension, never accepting structures' evil expressions as "necessary," and always applauding and supporting the expressions of light when they appear.

The emotions related to rebellion are a part of your life for substantial reasons. Understand them and go forward in the grace of Jesus as you court his church.

The second word that brings to the surface certain emotions is *parenting*. We must recognize that many people aspire to positions of leadership because they gain their sense of security through the control of others. Their little empires become "successful" as these leaders increase the size of their faithful following. Typically they will insist on thinking for you (although they won't say it as blatantly as that), and they will instill in you a fear of other points of view. You stop investigating life for yourself and, in fact, stop using your God-given mind. These leaders feed especially on sincere young Christians and broken or crushed Christians. You are particularly vulnerable to them because they communicate the desire to care for you, to fix all your problems, to protect you from the destructive influences "out there." They also take advantage of Christians who have been underexposed to the variety of doctrinal views within orthodox Christianity.

Stay away from these leaders. Your presence only massages their egos and even lends legitimacy to their actions. As a result, their empires will grow all the more, and they will abuse a greater number of people. They have the audacity to assume "parental" control over you. I hear the language of "parenting" often in evangelical/fundamentalist discipling organizations whose staff assume a maternalistic, paternalistic role over students. The biblical concept of discipleship allows no place for that sort of control. Other forms of "parenting" may be expressed with words such as "my congregation," "my students," "my people." People who overuse possessive language may be betraying a sense that they have the right to own you. There is only one rightful owner: God.

The number of options taken out of your life, the degree to which your world is shrinking, will reveal the level of unwholesome control through "parenting." "Parenters" want to limit the exposure others bring to you so they themselves will be your primary influence. Your circle of friends will grow small, your genuine contact with non-Christians and other views of Christian living will decrease, you will begin to suspect those outside your camp as foul-motived, and you will become increasingly paranoid of great schemes hatched against you by the "secular humanists" and "liberal press."

Leaders who genuinely care about you will *enlarge* your world, increase your exposure to others' views, invite your criticisms of their own ways, lessen their input to your worldview and discipleship process (while encouraging you to be influenced by others) —and will in fact *learn* from you. They will help your world become less black and white and more ambiguous, they will inspire you to risk where you've never been before, and when you return you will lead them down paths that are new to their Christian experience.

Finally, we will keep bumping into the word *accountability.* This has the potential of being another controlling mechanism, whereby you feel spiritually pressured to submit your brains and life to a group of people whose opinions are supposed to hold some heavenly authority over you. Most often it is the pastor, head of an organization, or campus staff leader calling for you to be accountable. Too often what such a leader is actually seeking is your obedience and subservience. You want to be wise: Your vulnerability resulted in pain in the first place. Don't allow false guilt to propel you back to the place of abuse. God has given you a mind and set of experiences that make up your unique life. You have the gift of being able to hear the Holy Spirit.

True accountability is actually friendship-in-action. It implies no control or spiritual authority. Accountability is that collection of deepening relationships with those who listen carefully to your life and then, because of earned trust, are able to respond honestly and lovingly to your circumstances. Control is neither desired nor implied. You listen to them and conclude in the environment of dignity and freedom how you shall live your life. Perhaps the most common form of accountability in my generation is what transpires when friends casually get together and talk about their lives. Ideas are exchanged, cautions ventured, honesty freely dealt out, advice offered when welcomed, love given where pain breaks the heart, and prayers made for each other's success in following Jesus. Real accountability is one of your best friends, and a wise person would nurture the relationships in which deep love and a profound dignity reign.

So, the tentative courtship with the church has begun. Now we turn to the rewards.

24

Friendship in the Faith

The good news about the church is that it is best understood in the context of truest friendships. Church is not primarily a structure or organization that is represented by formal offices (pastor, elder, deacon, and the like) or specific sacraments (such as Communion); rather, at its heart it is people who in relation to each other are a visible illustration of the family of God.

Jesus takes the disciples through a series of images to describe his relationship to them. At one level the disciples have the obligatory title of "slave." Not very flattering, but doctrinally sound. They are owned by Creator Yahweh and cannot claim independence; they are literally God's possession. All of their life is to be lived in submission to their master's design and will. The issue of "lordship" is primary. What we have here is a stark obedience orientation, a relationship to which the notions of joy, fellowship, fulfillment, and companionship are quite tangential.

At another level Jesus describes his disciples as coworkers. Now there is a certain camaraderie implied with the Creator. We have a "co-creative" role, one with a board-room aura: Let's get down to planning together, figure out how to save this old world. Our relationship permits some discussion, some give-and-take, rather than being strictly hierarchical and authoritarian. What brings us together has to do not so much with each other as with something external, out there, that needs fixing. We have come together to accomplish a task. This parallels the relationship between employees of specialized ministries that, for example, plant churches or feed the hungry.

Both the "slave" and "coworker" titles apply to us still. God has not given up the sovereign throne, and still invites us into the partnership of blessing others with the good news of the kingdom. But Jesus tells his disciples that there is much more. They are also his friends. They have actually come to that point of caring about *each other*, of enjoying each other's company and desiring more of it. I believe that one day we will witness the curious phenomenon of Jesus being reunited with his buddies-of-earth. Their good times will be retold to each other, and the friendship will pick right up where it had been left off several thousand years earlier. What has transpired between Jesus and the disciples is a deep friendship that is best described with the word "love." This is the heart of Christian fellowship, "friendship in the faith."

As I struggle with the reality of my own failures and pain, I am blessed to have a few friends whom I truly love and who truly love me. It is fair to say we desire each other. Such a mystical meeting point perhaps is clear to me only as I compare it to a similar mystical bond I have with my spouse. There are a few human beings with whom I am in love. And there are a few others who are moving into that circle. I believe we have touched something that is fundamental to an understanding of the Trinity, the heavenly model, and the church, the earthly expression. We have been wrapped together in the tenderness of the Holy Spirit, regarding the other as higher than ourselves, as precious treasure. We bring to each other the comfort that Christ intended the family to give; we encourage, exhort, honor, forgive, enjoy, and struggle. Dignity reigns between. Yes, you could say that we have seen Jesus in the other and we adore his creation.

I hope this does not sound too much like a mushy story. It is a love story, and it is the story that has emerged through the crucible of life's cruel, near-unbearable assaults on our souls. We have picked each other up from the gutter many times, we have applied salve to the wounds, we have nursed to the early hours of the morning, we have prayed desperately for the other's survival, we have entered into the other's hell and have emerged together singed by the scorching flames.

And why not? Is this not love, to lay down one's life for a brother or sister?

Thank God for the friend who loves at all times. This is the family into which we are invited. In your journey out of pain, this is the body of Jesus to you. Those formal events—Sunday-morning service, committees, special programs—may be excellent expressions of the body at work, but they are all too distant and fast-paced to be your true friends. God has created us to need each other. When God created Adam, the result was a perfectly lonely man. No amount of the Garden of Eden in its original splendor was able to satisfy the need of Adam for . . . what was it? He didn't know what he needed, but when God provided Eve it was immediately clear that she was perfect. Companionship. Friendship. These are part of our very nature.

As you venture back to the family of Christ, take comfort in your friends—the one, two, or more people who love you dearly, whom you love dearly. They are the heart of the body of Christ to you, the gift of the gospel.

It is painful to have been betrayed by friends in the process of ministry. Initially there is no lonelier experience than to discover that certain relationships were actually nothing more than convenient alliances for the attainment of some sort of ministry goal. But on the other side of this harrowing valley of death is the cementing of true friendships that perhaps would not have been known to us except for the rejection experience. Activists, especially, are surprised to find that their best friends are not those who were partners in ministry, but those who loved at all times. Vulnerable church members discover that their true friends are not the clergy who are paid to do the work of the kingdom, but those who love simply because they are friends.

We learn from the story of Adam and Eve that we are not a duality, a battleground between body and spirit. Our God-created humanity is such an intertwining of spirit and flesh that human friendship is a profoundly spiritual experience. Friendship is perhaps the best picture of the kingdom the world will see. All of us have many acquaintances, but there are not too many who are friends in the deepest sense.

We will discover, ultimately, that people are what the kingdom is all about. Programs come and go, but people remain forever. Our recovery from pain will be evidenced in part as we gain a determined commitment to people linked to a tentative commitment to programs. No project will make it to our excitement zone if we perceive it to be injurious to others. Plans to build a new sanctuary or to launch a new evangelistic effort will have little worth to us if their implementation requires the sacrifice of people.

God has made us for community. We simply are not able to thrive outside of mature, growing relationships. We need the gifts they give to us, they need the gifts we bring to them. As we benefit from a strong base of friendships in the community of faith, we will find courage to venture out into other relationships with people unlike ourselves and into relationships in which the difficult work of forgiving and struggling for unity will be primary. We will begin to broaden our perception of the family, because as we venture out we will find beauty in the diversity of God's prized creation. It will be as though we had lived our entire lives on white Wonder Bread. We were sadly undernourished. Now we sit at the banquet spread of people who suggest the stunning glory of thousands of glistening fluorescent fish in a South Pacific reef. Our once cramped and marginal visions of the family, sadly marred by ill-treatment, have been transformed into a playground of friendships and discoveries of God's lavish gifts to us.

Our newfound ability to delight in the family of God is an indication that we are becoming whole people again. The healing balm of the Comforter has been effective in our souls, and a certain tenderness is returning to our spirit. Thank God for friends who have been the incarnation of Jesus to us in this most wretched and trying season. We never really suspected that relief would come, but it did. Our lives are being transformed, miraculously, into the reconciled, loving community of Jesus, and the fragrance of love is extending its irresistible pull to others, who now look upon us with wonder and ask how they might enter through the door.

25

Live with Dignity

Our final assault on the evil committed against us, strange as it may first seem, is to live a life of dignity.

This is the upside-down nature of the kingdom to which we belong. The degree of pain that we feel from abuse is most likely a measure of the injustice committed against us. Our outrage, in part, reflects the fact that we *know* we are made with dignity and therefore should not be demeaned or abused. We now have the opportunity to turn that outrage into an act of God: We can determine to treat others with dignity.

That response will not be our first or our natural inclination. We will more likely partly withdraw into the "I am a rock" zone of safety or become harsh and cynical about anything good; we are more prone to become the sort of beast that attacked us, repaying to the world "out there" evil for evil. But there is a higher and more noble way, and because of God's healing work in our soul, we can aspire to it.

We have the option of going to bed every night with the satisfaction of having lived that day with dignity—the satisfaction of choosing better over worse, love over hatred, tenderness over death, hope over cynicism. I am not talking of some doctrinal view of life but rather a decision to carefully and deliberately live each day in a manner that reflects the dignity I have come to accept in myself and all God's people. We are talking about a revolutionary concept that subverts the designs against the souls of this whole world. We are speaking of turning evil on its head.

No grand scheme here of reaching every person in the world with the love of God or feeding all the hungry, but rather an intentional lifestyle of treating each person we encounter with dignity, one by one, a little at a time, reflecting the biblical call to treat everyone with the sort of love we want to be dealt to us.

The most lovely and unexpected outcome of this simple act of dignity is that as we deal it out, we ourselves become filled with a dignity that no one can take from us. We, by our love, give to others what was missing for us. And we receive in return a hundredfold—not from them, but from the very act of dignity itself. This is the wild nature of dignity. In essence, dignity takes care of its own.

When I moved to the United States from South Africa, the question that most plagued me was, "What exactly does it mean to be a Christian?" I have loving and thoughtful parents who were careful to instill in me the truths related to the gift of sins forgiven and eternal peace in the presence of Jesus. My problem, however, was that I was reared in a country that had the world's highest percentage of churchgoers and yet one of the most evil systems of government on earth (a system created and perpetuated in God's name). How could we claim to have the love of God in us while we continued purposefully to destroy the lives and families of our black brothers and sisters? Oh, there were always crafty anthropological arguments and excuses offered for the ill-treatment, but the honest bottom line was that blacks were not being loved as we would want to be loved. In other words, we were not living out the gospel.

And yet I did not know one government or church leader who disagreed with Bill Bright's "Four Spiritual Laws." It appeared that all were at peace with themselves and God for having recited the little prayer at the end of the booklet. Without question, that simple little gospel presentation became their permission to continue the abuse of blacks. This fact of my upbringing drew me into a crisis of faith when I left home. I had to return to the Scriptures to discover afresh what a Christian really is.

To my surprise, I found the Bible to be less clear on exactly how one becomes a Christian than it was on what the Christian life is. As I read through the Scriptures, I was born again to a deeper faith in the discovery that all the requirements of "the law and the prophets" are summed up in two great laws: that we love the Lord with all our heart, soul, mind, and strength and that we love our neighbor as ourselves. And, says the book of Romans, "love does no harm to its neighbor."

Aha!

You don't have to be racist to be a Christian. Strange discovery, you might think, but for one who grew up in the church-run apartheid system, a marvelously freeing concept.

I am now of the opinion that it does not matter so much to receive the approval of the religious systems. Their approval ratings are far too often connected to the propagation of their structures. Sometimes you have to be immoral to gain their approval: Be antiwoman, be deceptive about the historical roots of our nation, be racist, ignore the abuses against members who don't see the political issues just our way, ignore the oppressed—and the list goes on. The system would train us to forgo the finer points of Christian living in exchange for club membership.

We have the privilege of saying no to all that, of finding acceptance in a profound encounter with Christ, of learning that our self-image and worth are not connected to the goodwill of the system. We have been taught dignity by Christ, and now we are returning that gift of dignity to the world. As our commitment to the family of faith grows, we find ourselves drawn to others who are also exploring the notion of treating others with the same dignity Christ has dealt to us. For us it is a journey, and we all feel like beginners who know very little. But our rich experience of fellowship with others under the dignified banner of Christ is building up our faith, and we are finding courage to join together in organized ways (structures!) in order to live our new corporate life for the benefit of those still crushed by the world's machinery.

Ultimately this is our freedom—to move daily in the world with dignity. To say yes to the truth at every turn, and no to the lies. We do not have to repeat the patterns that deny people their worth (as we were denied). Instead, we can become absolutely free, because there is no rule or law that can prevent us from believing in our dignity or from treating others with dignity. That is the maddening truth of the gospel at its best, and that is what the church can offer the world. It begins, of course, in our treatment of each other and finally extends to those outside the faith who wait for the same good news.

It will not be enough, then, to "act Christian," because the label "Christian" carries with it baggage, all sorts of prejudices and religious perversions. No, we act *human* toward each other, in the most profoundly spiritual sense of that word. And if the club decides to let us in, it is not our resting place or good fortune, it is simply another location in which to treat people with dignity.

26

Freedom to Love:
Returning to the Pain

So, here we are at the end of our exploration of pain. We have looked together at its causes, we have cried our rage and sorrow at its brutal wounds, we have searched for possible remedies, and we have dared to hope for renewed energy and fellowship.

We are different people. Thank God that in the process of unfolding our pain we have been freed from religion. We cannot accept that the purpose of our pain was to lead us to this point, because then we have conceded the most horrifying of notions—that evil is conceived in the heart of a good God. No, evil is just that, evil. But thank God, we have somehow found Jesus in our pain, and we are free to live as dignified people who are no longer lured by the shallow world of religion.

There is, I believe, one final stage in the progress toward our triumph.

Jesus wants to turn us outward to discover the devastating pain of the world. Because we have found Jesus to be with us in our pain—we are, as it were, at home with our pain—we now find ourselves gifted through our own trauma and darkness to reach out and offer a hand to others in the cage of pain. Integrity reminds us that we are unable to say why others are experiencing their darkness, but we have found one in that darkness who went through the valley with us. We have discovered ourselves converted to that love. We now love because we have been loved. In that loving we have encountered reality and find ourselves at peace with ourselves and our world. We have found what the unloved—be they churched or unchurched—are desperately seeking.

Jesus calls us to happily and freely give them the gift of love-in-the-pain.

We must accept one inescapable conclusion about this world: It is a miserably cruel place that retains very little of what the book of Genesis tells us was its original nature. There is nothing perfect about this place—and, in fact, very little good in it. This must become part of our working definition of reality. Just because we do good to others the world is not necessarily going to do good to us. Indeed, we must count on the opposite. It's a strange thing that we usually accept the prophets once they have left, but only rarely while they are with us. And because we follow Jesus, the one who without question lived a perfect and sinless life, we cannot expect less than what he received at the hands of Caesar and the religious establishment of his day.

When Jesus' healing work is near completion in us, it is not measured by the number of answers we have to the wretched condition of this world; it is more accurately measured by our desire to become tenderness to the unanswered and broken people of the world. If the church has any role in society, it is to leave its pulpit behind and to lock itself inside the cages of pain, to become the living incarnation of Jesus Christ and minister to those who suffer—to minister out of the profound understanding of what it is like to grow up in the cage.

This is where the church will gain its integrity, this is where it begins to reflect its true function. From this life in the cage, the church can have a truly compassionate, biblical, and effective response to the world's ills. I will venture to say that ten years from now, the church that has learned to enter the cages of pain, to suffer with those who suffer, to touch the pain of a devastated generation, to *live in the pain,* will be the church that is widely known. This will be the church that is growing wildly. It will not be marked by superstructures and seminars on how to grow your middle-class club in the suburbs; rather, it will have the reputation of providing a sanctuary for pain, a place where the marginalized, beaten, crushed, lonely, and despairing have found a home and healing. These churches will have learned to avoid silly theological formulations that have no actual connection to those who suffer—theological concepts brewed in the classrooms of seminaries and Bible schools, far from the hurting crowd.

We have discovered that our life is a cage of pain. To our relief, we have also discovered that Christ lives inside our cage of pain. And now we are calling for the church to intentionally become an institution that might be best described as the "church inside the cage." No other institution could better reflect the incarnation of Jesus.

I used to live in a little community called Northwest Pasadena. Unfortunately, it had a very high crime rate, linked to unemployment, lack of education, drugs, and poverty. As is too often the case, whites had left the neighborhood in virtual droves when people of other ethnic backgrounds began to move in. The white churches abandoned the area and prayed to God to bless their efforts to put up new sanctuaries in the "safe" all-white suburbs. And, of course, church members were harangued to put their money with the priorities of the kingdom—in other words, help finance the new buildings removed from the pain of the world.

Yet the white churches never forgot about our little neighborhood, where a specialized police force of eighteen vehicles was established just for our safety. From time to time these white churches that left our area send in their evangelism teams. They have no idea of the pain that makes up our existence, but nonetheless they come with their prepackaged literature and notions of good news.

You must understand that we have it backwards. The Scripture says that it is exceedingly difficult for a rich man to enter the kingdom of heaven. His riches will come between him and the costly demands of God. But we have distorted the gospel, made it into a middle-class concept: Becoming a Christian now simply means signing on for some benefits. This is how it goes: Successful and wealthy Joe Businessman has a family, a secure job, a house (he owns it), and a good future. Of course he's happy, but he's not fulfilled because he doesn't have Jesus. Along comes a witnessing team that explains to him that he never can have real fulfillment unless Jesus is in his heart, and that in fact he can live for all eternity if he will simply ask Jesus to forgive him of all his sins.

Not a bad deal from a businessman's point of view. That Saturday afternoon Joe says the prayer, and Monday he goes back to work, ready to enjoy his secure job, house, family, and heaven to boot. The gospel was an excellent addition to his already cushy life.

Come to Northwest Pasadena. I have watched the witnessing teams show up after they have prayed to God to help them in their evangelistic raids. They jump out of their vans and go door to door to tell us that all we need is the sinner's prayer: Say the words, and Jesus will take care of all your problems and save you from hell. So my neighbors listen to the pitch.

What these evangelists don't understand is that many of my neighbors are single mothers, recovering drug addicts, parents without enough money to feed their children, and aliens who are unemployed and unable to master English. Some go through the degrading ritual of selling their bodies for cash to buy food, and others face the threat of a landlord who wants to evict them for not staying current with the rent. For these neighbors, the sinner's prayer does not change any of their difficult circumstances. Mormons and Jehovah's Witnesses come through the neighborhood offering a similar quick-fix to life's ills.

What none of the evangelists understands is that the neighborhood is caught in an unjust system perpetuated by the powerful white middle class of Pasadena, many of whom are members of the white churches that send witnessing teams to our neighborhood. Apparently their good news of Jesus does not have a whole lot to do with our neighborhood's pain.

I hope you are outraged by the church that insists on escaping the world's pain. I hope you never let go of the trauma you knew in your most desperate moments. I pray to God that you will have the vision and grace to live in the middle of the world's pain, to absorb its harsh and smashing blows on the priceless creatures of Jesus. I pray that you and I will become providers of tenderness in the cage, ministers of dignity, messengers of hope and courage. That is what my neighborhood experienced, by the way, through Christians who moved into the area, into their pain, and now minister to them out of a profound understanding of their torment.

I pray God that as this world's people scream their agony against the prison walls of their existence, they will look and see our tears for their pain, they will feel our arms about their weak and ravaged bodies, they will drink—to being drunk—the wine that has filled our souls, they will feel the scars in our tortured flesh, and in their darkest hours they will join the dance in the cage, where to their surprise they discover the tenderhearted Jesus, the biggest party animal of us all.

By the way, Michelle, the drug addict and prostitute of whom I wrote in the beginning of this book, found the tenderhearted Jesus.

The sky turned dark and mocked us with the death of hope on Friday. But we know better now. We celebrate our freedom as we watch the tombstone roll away. It's Sunday, and the serpent's head is crushed beyond recognition. No one rushes to its aid. And as the party draws to its close at three in the morning, the janitor sweeps snakeskin into the trash—trampled, apparently, by the dancing in the cell. And outside the cage you notice prisonkeepers sipping their tea and exchanging abstruse doctrinal concepts on the redemption of the human race.

You laugh yourself to sleep.